The Jew of Seville

Frontispiece: Victor Séjour, from *Diogène,* Mar. 8, 1857.
Cliché Bibliothèque nationale de France, Paris.

The Jew of Seville

VICTOR SÉJOUR

Translated from the French by
Norman R. Shapiro

Introduction by M. Lynn Weiss

University of Illinois Press
Urbana and Chicago

Manufactured in the United States of America
c 5 4 3 2 1

∞ This book is printed on acid-free paper.

This translation of Victor Séjour's *Diégarias* has been approved by the Longfellow Institute, Harvard University.

Library of Congress Cataloging-in-Publication Data
Séjour, Victor, 1817–1874.
[Diégarias. English]
The Jew of Seville / Victor Séjour ; translated from the French by
Norman R. Shapiro ; introduction by M. Lynn Weiss.
p. cm.
Includes bibliographical references.
ISBN 0-252-02700-0 (cloth : alk. paper)
I. Shapiro, Norman R. II. Title.
PQ3939.S3D5413 2002
842'.8—dc21 2001003139

To the memory of Nathan Irvin Huggins

Contents

Acknowledgments

MANY THANKS TO MATT CALIHMAN AND LANYA LAMOURIA for truly exceptional research assistance; and for their patient and expert guidance, I am grateful to the librarians at the Bibliothèque Nationale. Special thanks are due Willis Regier for his enthusiastic support of the project. My heartfelt thanks to Werner Sollors, who led me to Victor Séjour. I am most grateful to Norman Shapiro, whose brilliant English translation has given this play new life.

—M. Lynn Weiss

Translator's Preface

NORMAN R. SHAPIRO

EVERY LITERARY TRANSLATOR IS FACED, SIMPLISTICALLY speaking, with basic problems of content and form: the need to bring across—literally, to "trans-late"—the ideas clothed in one language into another, and to do so, insofar as possible, in a "clothing" whose style is not at odds with that of the original. I think most translators accept that principle as a given; and, in a traditionally unappreciated craft in which personal creative satisfaction is the major, if not the only, driving force, that satisfaction derives from the measure of success achieved in following it through to the finished product.

The translator of theater has an additional problem. While, for me, all literature is meant to be recited aloud and heard, or ought to be, fiction and poetry, at least, can be enjoyed in the privacy of one's armchair with nothing but an inner soundtrack bringing the words to life. (Much literature, in fact—modern hermetic poetry is a good case in point—almost demands such personal readings and, indeed, rereadings, silent or aloud, for its "meaning" to emerge.) But, though plays too can certainly be read and appreciated in silence, and while, practically speaking, many must be, since we cannot possibly attend performances of every play we would like to experience—especially at today's prices, if for no other logistical reason—we should not forget that they are, nonetheless, written to be *acted.* That is, seen and heard. The conscientious translator tries to bear this in mind. A possible exception is the case of a translation intended strictly as a scholarly document, reflecting the political, social, or intellectual milieu—or all three—of its period, and with no theatrical ambitions; destined for archive and dissertation rather than for the footlights. But in the best of all possible worlds even such work, it seems to me, if it purports to be "theater," should bear some relation to dramatic art.

Another exception is the modern-dress theatrical adaptation and similar intentional reworkings. But if the "clothing" is updated—the decor, dialogue, and allusions modernized—a certain stylistic unity is essential in such transformations too. Unless, that is, parody or comic effect in general is aimed at. Most of us, for example, would shy away from translating, say, a seventeenth-century Racine tragedy with a helter-skelter mix of high classical vocabulary and twentieth- (or twenty-first-) century slang, or of elegant verse and doggerel. Nor would our serious version call for characters in togas crossing the stage on skateboards. Not that there isn't a place for such inspired liberties. But they are, obviously, the stuff of comedy, and the translators—or adapters—who indulge in them must be clear on what they are attempting to present to their spectator/reader.

In preparing an English version of Victor Séjour's *Diégarias*, I have followed these principles, though not without confronting a number of problems and choices. The original, a mid-nineteenth-century drama of heroic dimensions, is in a rhymed verse that respects the various strictures that the genre imposed on Séjour and his theatrical contemporaries, not the least among them Victor Hugo. A glance at some of the latter's texts—the well-known *Ruy Blas* is a good example—will show the prosodic conventions that obtained. At the outset, therefore, I had to decide the basic question: would I use prose or verse? The former could certainly convey the content, but would it "clothe" it appropriately and establish a tone analogous to that of the original? The latter, on the other hand, could, if I were not careful and judicious, inadvertently veer the text toward the comic. Then too, if I opted for verse, need it be metered and rhymed? After all, blank verse drama in English is, to say the very least, respectable; and even a free-verse adaptation could be contextually faithful and aesthetically effective.

I would like to be able to say that my eventual choice of formal verse was dictated solely by adherence to principle: the desire to produce an effect as close as I could to Séjour's original. The truth of the matter, however, is that, as a translator, I thrive on the challenge a text poses; and, while a prose version of *Diégarias* would pose many, a verse translation in rhyming couplets would pose far more. Especially if I wanted to avoid the singsong effect one risks falling into when using iambic pentameter, the canonical substitute for the traditional 12-syllable French alexandrine. The reader will see that I have tried to reconcile the polar opposites of strict form and flexible liberty, maintaining the one while subjecting it to the other, thanks to such expedients as broken lines, inserted interjections, displaced stresses, and liberal use of enjambment, all characteristic of Séjour's French contemporaries and even, to some extent, their classical predecessors. The challenge was to do all that in a language that was not jarringly modern and that, to come back to my first concern, could be convincingly brought to the stage and acted, albeit as an example of the somewhat bombastic elegance of its own, not my own, artistic and theatrical period.

Séjour himself, it must be said, did not make the task of actability and staging as easy as he might have done. With very little of the exact, almost compulsive, scenic precision that one finds in most French romantic dramas, produced for the eye as well as for the ear, he keeps his stage directions to a minimum, seldom troubling to indicate all the entrances the set contains in a given act, all the necessary furnishings and props, and even, on occasion, seeming to contradict himself. I have taken the liberty of regularizing all this as best I can, supplementing the directions where it seemed advantageous to do so. Needless to say, any experienced director will have his or her own ideas, and will see fit to delete, alter, or add to them accordingly. I have, however, preserved the author's gallicization of most of the Spanish names, with the understandable exception of "Don Juan." (Who, after all, would dream of turning him into a "Don Jean"?) Though taking the liberty of changing "Perès" to "Pérez," I have resisted hispanizing "Henri" to "Enrique," "Sanche" to "Sancho," et alia. Though the action and decor are Spanish, the original text is French, and an English version should, I think, retain that fiction without straining to the breaking point the spectator/reader's suspended disbelief.

My most striking and immediately obvious liberty is in my change of the title, keeping its Spanishness while alluding pointedly to the play's subject. Perhaps one can object that it reveals too much of the plot too soon. But I think that the curiosity it evokes justifies the trade-off, and hope that it speaks more eloquently than the original to today's potential audiences.

Introduction

M. LYNN WEISS

LONG BEFORE THE HARLEM RENAISSANCE, THE ARTISTIC achievements of Louisiana's francophone, antebellum free Creoles of color contested the popular opinion that people of African origins were incapable of producing art. Indeed the first anthology of literature by Americans of African descent was a collection of poetry by seventeen of Louisiana's free men of color. *Les Cenelles: choix de poésies indigènes* was published in 1845 in New Orleans, the same year in which *The Narrative of the Life of Frederick Douglass* appeared.[1] *Les Cenelles* was an extraordinarily self-conscious gesture by writers who did not want their work to simply "pass" into anthologies of French literature, and our understanding of American literature is incomplete if we do not include such texts in our study of the field. But unlike Douglass's *Narrative, Les Cenelles* is a volume of romantic poetry, and this has prompted critics to conclude that the relatively privileged writers it represents produced little that addressed slavery or racism, therefore little of interest to readers today.[2] Yet some of their writing was infused with and informed by the conflict of race in the United States. The difficulties these writers faced as people of color is inscribed in the volume's title; "cenelles" are the indigenous hawthorn berries that grow in varying shades on the shrub's thorny branches. Among the contributors to *Les Cenelles* was Victor Séjour, one of mid-nineteenth-century Paris's popular playwrights.[3]

For an American playwright, Victor Séjour's career was remarkable, but for an American of African descent it was extraordinary. When Séjour was only twenty-six years old, his first play, *Diégarias*

(*The Jew of Seville*), was accepted by the venerable Comédie Française (still known in 1843 as the Théâtre Français). Twenty of his twenty-two plays were produced between 1844 and 1875, and in one season Séjour had three plays in production simultaneously. His work was reviewed by France's best drama critics, including Théophile Gautier, the Goncourt brothers, Félix Savard, and Jules Janin. And some of the era's finest actors, Marie Laurent, Frédérick-Lemaître, and Lia Félix, performed in his plays. Napoleon III attended opening night of *La Tireuse de cartes* (*The Fortune-Teller*) and *Les Massacres de la Syrie* (*The Syrian Massacres*). And in 1874, Victor Séjour's death was reported by Reuters, the *Times* (London), and the *New Orleans Times,* as well as by *L'Abeille de la Nouvelle-Orléans.*[4] Séjour's success in Paris was countered by the grudging recognition it received back in New Orleans. Even though *The Jew of Seville* was performed in his native city, a proposal to award the young playwright a medal for his success provoked a stir because of his race.[5]

In his lifetime, Victor Séjour published an elegy, "Le Retour de Napoléon," a short story, "The Mulatto," and the first half of a serialized novel, *Le Comte de Haag.*[6] In addition to the twenty-two plays he had completed, Séjour was reportedly working on another, *L'Esclave* (*The Slave*), but it has never been found.[7] In 1861, *Douglass' Monthly* reported that Séjour was preparing a play based on the life of John Brown.[8] The remarkable range of his work is suggested by the contrast between the abolitionist tale "The Mulatto" and the drawing-room comedy *Le Paletot brun* (*The Brown Overcoat*). Formally and thematically Séjour's plays ranged from classical five-act dramas in verse, such as *The Jew of Seville,* to the spectacular melodrama *Le Fils de la Nuit* (*Son of the Night*) or the controversial rendition of the infamous Mortara affair, *La Tireuse de cartes* (*The Fortune-Teller*).[9]

Well into the twentieth century, however, Victor Séjour's legacy had been preserved chiefly in French literary histories and biographies, or by historians of Creole Louisiana such as Rodolphe Lucien Desdunes and Charles Barthelemy Roussève.[10] Edward Laroque Tinker's 1932 literary biography, *Les Ecrits de langue française en Louisiane au dix-neuvième siècle,* included a lengthy discussion of Victor Séjour.[11] With the exception of a small essay on *Les Cenelles* in *Op-*

portunity in 1932, articles on Séjour's work began to appear in anglophone American journals only in the 1940s.[12] In an essay on the James Weldon Johnson Collection at Yale University, Carl Van Vechten noted that its holdings include seventeen of Séjour's plays.[13] In the centennial reprint of *Les Cenelles* in 1945, historian Edward Maceo Coleman's substantial introduction included a discussion of Séjour's work and career.[14] Scholarly articles and dissertations on Séjour infrequently appeared in the following decades. Then in 1972, Townsend Brewster translated Séjour's 1859 comedy, *The Brown Overcoat,* and it was produced that year at the Circle-in-the-Square Theater, as part of a bill of three one-act plays. Although reviews were mixed, this was the first English production of any Séjour play on the American stage.[15] James Hatch and Ted Shine included a translation of *The Brown Overcoat* in their 1974 anthology *Black Theatre USA.*[16] In 1986, Victor Séjour was included in the volume on African American writers before the Harlem Renaissance in *Dictionary of Literary Biography,* and in 1990 *Early Black American Playwrights* included an entry on Séjour.[17] Charles Edwards O'Neill published a substantial article on Séjour's plays in 1979 and his comprehensive biography, *Séjour: Parisian Playwright of Louisiana,* appeared in 1995.[18] The first English translation of Victor Séjour's short story "The Mulatto" was published in the *Norton Anthology of African American Literature* in 1997.[19] Writer Andrea Lee's translation of "The Mulatto" appeared in *The Multilingual Anthology of American Literature* in 2000.[20] This volume is the only English translation of Victor Séjour's first play, *Diégarias* (*The Jew of Seville*).[21] In addition, *Les noces vénitiennes* (1855) was presented in English as *Outlaw of the Adriatic; or, The Female Spy and the Chief of Ten* in 1859. *La Tireuse de cartes* (*The Fortune-Teller*) was adapted as *The Woman in Red* by Joseph Stirling Coyne in 1872. To appreciate the scope of Victor Séjour's remarkable career, we must consider where he began.

Victor Séjour was born into the Creole-of-color community of New Orleans in 1817, five years after Louisiana became part of the United States. Louisiana's history as a Spanish and then a French territory had an important impact on the way slaves and free persons of color were perceived and treated. Evidence of this is apparent in the *Code noir,* a set of laws designed to regulate the lives of slaves in the French colonies under Louis XIV. According to Caryn Cossé Bell, the *Code noir* recognized the "moral personality" of slaves in that it required that they be instructed in the teachings of the Catholic church and that they be baptized, married, and buried in the church. Slaves were forbidden to work on Sundays and other Catholic holy days.[22] Even though it was a violation of the *Code noir,* the church did perform interracial marriages.[23] Indeed the origins of the racial mixture that came to be known as Creole of color are traceable to the early eighteenth century, when French and Spanish colonists often took slave women as mistresses or wives, freed them, and recognized and raised their children.[24] Victor Séjour's grandfather Marcou Latour was white and his grandmother Magdelaine Sterlin was a free woman of color from San Domingue.[25] The legacy of French and Spanish colonialism made the status of Louisiana's free Creoles of color an extraordinary exception to the experience of free blacks in the antebellum United States.

Among the approximately ten thousand refugees from the Haitian revolution, Louis Séjour, Victor's father, arrived in New Orleans in 1809. Between 1810 and 1830 the population of the free Creoles of color quadrupled from 4,000 to 16,710.[26] These new immigrants contributed to an already stable and prosperous community. By 1830 members of this group owned sugar and cotton plantations and slaves; others owned small businesses, worked as carpenters, tailors, iron smiths, or printers, or entered professions such as medicine or architecture. Their children were educated in private schools: in 1850, an astounding four-fifths of this community were literate and had over a thousand children in school. By 1860, Louisiana's Creole-of-color community owned property worth fifteen million dollars.[27] But this community developed and prospered on the periphery of an increasingly polarized society, occupying a precarious position between francophone white Creoles and anglophone Americans, between black and white, between free and slave.

The Séjour family lived in the heart of the French Quarter in the Vieux Carré neighborhood. Séjour's father was a merchant who owned a small dry goods store. Young Victor attended Michel Séligny's Sainte Barbe Academy for the children of the wealthier families in the community, as did another *Les Cenelles* poet, Camille

Thierry. Between 1834 and 1836, Victor Séjour, like many of his peers, left New Orleans for Paris, probably to complete his formal education. There is no record of his having matriculated anywhere; instead, Séjour's first published piece, the short story "The Mulatto," appeared in 1837 in *Revue des colonies.*[28] In 1841 Séjour published *Le Retour de Napoléon* to honor the interment of Napoleon's remains at Les Invalides. The success of Séjour's elegy (later published in *Les Cenelles*) gave him an introduction to playwright Emile Augier and, more importantly, to his lifelong hero—novelist, playwright, and fellow *homme de couleur,* Alexandre Dumas (père).

When Victor Séjour arrived in Paris, the social and political chaos provoked by the Revolution and Napoleon's rise to power had begun to change French theater. As a result of the Revolution, French theaters had been democratized and eventually were declared free of state control in 1791. But for Napoleon there was entirely too much freedom, and in 1807 the state recognized and subsidized only four official theaters, but regardless of venue, every play had to be approved by government censors. The repertoire of the official theaters was restricted to the classics, while the secondary "popular" theaters received no state funding, leaving them vulnerable to the vagaries of the marketplace. Popular theater included vaudeville, melodrama, pantomime, and "féerie," the spectacular melodrama, light on plot and remarkable for its emphasis on fantastic scenery.[29] By the 1830s, the distinction between the repertoire of official and popular theaters had blurred, even though the restrictions on official theaters' repertoire were not formally abolished until 1864. Furthermore, over the first half of the nineteenth century, the population of Paris more than doubled, prompting an enormous demand for theatrical entertainment.

Victor Séjour's plays were featured in eight of the roughly two dozen popular theaters to flourish between 1830 and 1860. The span of his career coincided with important developments in French theater history. Audiences had become predominantly middle class; melodrama was in great demand; and new technologies had been developed that afforded greater use of special effects. By the 1840s, for example, because of developments in stage machinery and techniques, melodramatic plots became more complicated, requiring several scene changes and spectacular effects.[30] One of the most memorable plays of the 1856 season to take advantage of these new possibilities was Séjour's *Le Fils de la Nuit* (*Son of the Night*). Critic Théophile Gautier recalls the thrilling moment when the protagonist's ship "pitches on the backs of monstrous waves. Its prow dips and presses into the bitter troughs, soaking the forward sail, then rises and glistens . . . the sails flap, the ropes quiver . . . the storm redoubles its fury, the lightening multiplies its sulfurous flashes . . . soon the main mast cracks, totters and falls."[31] Many critics pronounced such innovations the death knell of the theater but they were hugely successful with audiences. *Le Fils de la Nuit* had an extraordinarily long run, from July of 1856 to January of 1857, and the box office receipts were correspondingly high.

Another development in French theater of this period was the great number of playwrights working in collaboration. Such collaboration had been rare in the eighteenth century, but the high demand for entertainment, the constant need for new productions, made it both commonplace and lucrative in the nineteenth century. For the first time in French theater history individual playwrights such as Victor Hugo and Alexandre Dumas (père) or actresses such as Rachel Félix and Sarah Bernhardt amassed fortunes; Dumas could even afford to pay for the construction of his own theater. Before the 1830s, authors were paid a lump sum for a play and a small fee for every night the play ran, and the fee did not correspond to box-office receipts. To insure a greater share of the profits and to protect dramatists from unscrupulous theater managers in Paris and the provinces, playwright Eugène Scribe founded the Société des auteurs dramatiques, which became one of the strongest trade unions in the city.[32] When Séjour's career began in 1843, membership in the society had become mandatory.

In this competitive and capricious world of mid-nineteenth-century French theater, Victor Séjour, a young Creole of color from New Orleans, had his first play accepted and performed by the Comédie Française. It was an extraordinary stroke of good luck. As one historian has argued, "There was hardly a single dramatist of note who did not, in the course of the century, approach the Comédie Française with the offer of one or the other of his works; to be performed on that historic stage was regarded as the crowning point of his career, tantamount to an official consecration."[33] One of the strengths of the

Comédie Française was that it was the only company with an effective reading committee functioning throughout the nineteenth century. After the postrevolutionary chaos, the company had reestablished its reading committee in 1803. Very like its prerevolutionary incarnation, the reading committee was made up of nine actors and actresses who, after a *viva voce* reading by the dramatist, would then decide whether or not to accept the play.[34] A dramatist who had never had a play performed at the Comédie Française (or, like Séjour, anywhere else) had a long way to go before meeting the committee. The preliminary steps were as follows: the dramatist was required to leave a copy of the play with the secretary, who then passed it along to one of the official readers; if the reader's report was positive, the play went on to an examining committee; if it cleared this hurdle, the play was then passed along to the reading committee. The proportion of plays submitted to those actually performed seems to have been generally low.[35] Séjour was especially fortunate in that *The Jew of Seville* was performed a mere eight months after having been accepted; Séjour's rival for stage time waited several years before his play's opening night.[36]

The Jew of Seville went through eleven performances in the summer of 1844, a respectable number for a debutant, and even though the play had its detractors, many of the reviews were quite favorable.[37] Théophile Gautier observed that the play was a success, and especially impressive for a first effort.[38] Though noting some flaws, the critic for *Illustration* concluded that Séjour's style was "energetic and concise."[39] The critic for the *Revue de Paris* argued that even though the play seemed dated, it clearly demonstrated the young playwright's promise: "We would willing say . . . 'The fruit is unripe, but it is there.' The playwright is M. Victor Séjour. He is young, and everything shows the poet in him."[40] The critics differed on the specific strengths and weakness of the play, but they agreed that the twenty-six-year-old novice was off to a strong start.

Drawing inspiration from the racial drama of Séjour's native land, *The Jew of Seville* dramatizes the theme of racial/religious persecution, the idea of passing, the difficulties of interfaith love and marriage, and the way such a polarized society makes it possible for parents to cause the deaths of their children. Séjour uses European anti-Semitism (the play is set in fifteenth-century Spain) to explore themes that are the mainstay of nineteenth-century African American literature. Séjour may have seen parallels between the conflict between blacks and Creoles of color with white America and the Jewish/Christian conflict because he perceived that for much of European history the conflict between Jews and Christians was more than simply a matter of faith. Moreover, the similarities between the experiences of European Jews and Creoles of color might have struck Séjour with special force because anti-Semitism had been written into the laws governing his native Louisiana. The first article of the *Code noir* expelled Jews from the colony: "The edict of the late King Louis XIV of glorious memory, of April 23, 1651, will be executed in our Province and Colony of Louisiana: in view of this we order from the said country all the Jews who may have established residence there whom, as declared enemies of the Christian name, we order to leave within three months starting with the day of publication of this document under penalty of confiscation of his person and possessions."[41] Ultimately, of course, Jews were tolerated in Catholic Louisiana, but it is significant that the code, designed to regulate the treatment of slaves, begins by designating the traditional Other for banishment. Victor Séjour's earliest treatment of this theme features the racially polarized milieu of plantation slavery. "The Mulatto" is the only work by Séjour that is set in the New World.[42]

"The Mulatto" first appeared in an abolitionist journal, *Revue des colonies,* the organ of a radical society of people of color. Published in Paris by Cyrille Bissette, an "homme de couleur" from Martinique, the *Revue* was dedicated to social justice and the abolition of slavery.[43] Set in San Domingue (or as the narrator reminds us, "now the Republic of Haiti"), "The Mulatto" is the familiar story of the mixed-race character whose one drop of black blood becomes a condemnation to an early grave. The theme appears repeatedly throughout the nineteenth century and into the twentieth, in texts such as Lydia Maria Child's "The Quadroons" (1842), William Wells Brown's *Clotel or: the President's Daughter* (1853), Dion Boucicault's *The Octoroon* (1859), Charles Chesnutt's "The Sheriff's Children" (1899); and Langston Hughes's "Father and Son" (1934) and that story's dramatic adaptation, *The Mulatto* (1935). Séjour's tale is remarkable not only because it appears so early (as far as we know, it is the first published short story by an American of African descent) but because of the economy and candor with which it renders the horror of chattel slavery.

Georges, the mulatto of the tale, is the son of a beautiful Senegalese woman and her brutal white master, Alfred. Georges grows up without knowledge of his father's identity. Years later, when Alfred attempts to rape Georges's wife Zélie, she resists and in the process, Alfred is injured. Georges pleads with Alfred to spare Zélie's life, noting that he has recently saved his master's life. Unmoved, Alfred invokes the *Code noir* and condemns Zélie to death. Georges escapes, but three years later he returns to murder Alfred and his wife and child. In the moment before his death, Alfred confesses that he is Georges's father; horrified by his crime, Georges then commits suicide. In nineteenth-century American literature, death is the predictable fate of the "tragic mulatto." But patricide is rare in early representations of this conflict between blood and clan. As Werner Sollors has observed, the patricide/suicide of the mulatto in this story connects the New World themes of slavery and "miscegenation" to the themes of Greek tragedy: complicated family relations, obscure origins, incest, and identity, and how these corrupt the family and ultimately society.[44]

In *The Jew of Seville,* a tragedy in the classical tradition, and later in the melodrama *The Fortune-Teller,* Séjour employs the New World's trope of the tragic mulatto to critique both Old and New World racism. Diégarias, the hero of the play, is in fact the Jew Jacob Eliacin, who through years of diligent and loyal service has become minister of the treasury to King Henry IV of Castile.[45] Some twenty years earlier, Eliacin had courted a young Christian noblewoman significantly named Bianca. When her uncle, Don Jacques de Tello, discovered this, he had Eliacin brought to his palace and beaten. Undeterred, the couple fled to Greece, where Bianca died after giving birth to their only child. Years later, a now-wealthy Jacob Eliacin returns to Seville as the non-Jew Diégarias with his daughter Inès, who does not know the truth of her origins. When the drama begins, the noblemen of Castile have plotted to overthrow the king, and among them is Don Juan de Tello, the son of Don Jacques and therefore Inès's cousin. Diégarias intercepts a letter by Don Juan wherein he boasts of having seduced Inès by marrying her in a sham ceremony. Diégarias insists that Don Juan marry his daughter, but seconds before he is to sign the marriage contract, with the king and nobles present, Don Juan reveals Diégarias's true identity and refuses to marry the Jew's daughter. The king and the nobles repudiate Diégarias, who retreats to his palace in humiliation and disgrace. Still, both the king and his enemies secretly solicit Diégarias to finance their separate armies. In exchange for Don Juan's death, Diégarias finances the king's army; he then funds the king's enemies. In the meantime, Inès, who still loves Don Juan, begs her father to rescind the death sentence. When he refuses, she arranges Don Juan's escape and poisons herself. Just as Diégarias believes he will have his revenge on both the king and Don Juan, he realizes that Inès is dying; the play ends with his cry: "I sought revenge but I have killed my child" (act 5, scene 8). As in "The Mulatto," the story ends with the "mulatto" character's death and, through her suicide, a form of patricide in that her death destroys her father at least figuratively.

One of the familiar themes Séjour employed in his characterization of the "mulatto" is the idea of racial Otherness as a form of physical and spiritual pollution. Don Juan refuses to marry Inès because a Jewish wife would dishonor his name and corrupt his soul (act 3, scene 8). Just as one drop of black blood was enough to make an apparently white person black, Inès's Jewish blood taints her noble Spanish blue blood. A similar theme appears in Dion Boucicault's extremely popular melodrama *The Octoroon* (1859). Zoe, the beautiful heroine, reveals to George Payton, her white suitor, why she cannot marry him: "Of the blood that feeds my heart, one drop in eight is black—bright red as the rest may be, that one drop poisons all the flood . . . I'm an unclean thing—forbidden by the laws—I'm an Octoroon!"[46]

In Spain the notion of "pure blood" and the possibility of pollution by the Other found its earliest expression in a special statute, *Sentencia-Estatuto,* adopted in Toledo in 1449. This statute prohibited Jewish *conversos* (converts from Judaism or Islam) from holding public office. Such practices culminated in the *limpieza de sangre* (purity of the blood) statutes in 1556.[47] Marc Shell has argued that these statutes were part of a nation-building process that began with the expulsion of the Jews in 1492 and of the Muslims in 1502.[48] The purity of blood statutes distinguished between "original" Christians and *conversos* based on heredity.[49] These statutes made it as impossible for a Jew or Muslim who had converted to Christianity (or their offspring) to be accepted by the "original" Christians as it was for a person of mixed ancestry to be anything but "black." Séjour seems to have underscored this parallel by setting his play in Seville shortly before 1492, the year that links Spain to America and, through the *limpieza de sangre,* Jews to the free people of color. He may have known that these laws were still in effect as he composed *The Jew of Seville;* they were not abolished until 1865.[50]

Like a congenital disease, this pollution is transmittable to children even if, like Inès, they are not raised Jewish (or if, like Zoe, it is impossible to know that they are black from their appearance). In fact Inès has been raised a Christian; indeed, at eighteen she has just learned that her father is a Jew. Moreover, according to Mosaic law, Inès is not a Jew because her mother Bianca was not a Jew, and according to the laws of the Catholic church Inès is a Christian. But no matter how white Zoe appears or how many times Inès is baptized, their perceived difference is fundamental to the identity and legitimacy of the "pure bloods" and so the contradiction remains unaddressed. How else to explain the legal fiction that for centuries supported the view "that white blood, though it can be wholly 'blackened' cannot be partly diluted."[51] In Sejour's native Louisiana up until 1970 a person with one thirty-second black ancestry was considered a "Negro."

After his public humiliation, Diégarias tells his daughter that a Jew is never at home in the Christian world. In rhetoric that explicitly describes the position of Séjour's Creole community in New Orleans, Diégarias warns Inès:

Today, we spoke of country, you
And I, and of the noble heroes, through
The ages, whom the past bequeaths to us.
But why? What folly is it to discuss
Such things! Is there a fatherland for those

Who have no rights? Tomorrow, if I chose
To put aside my pride and, humbly, go
Trembling before his Majesty... Bow low
And deep before our Christian King... Yes him
Whom I sustained, defended, life and limb,
For many a year... If I begged, on my knees,
Hands clasped in prayer: "O gentle monarch, please,
Help me! Many are they who now would seize
My wealth, my property... Who would divest
Me of my very life! Pray, save me, lest
I die anon!..." What think you would result?
Ah! How his rogues would mock me and exult
To chase away this Jew, so mad with pride,
That he knows not he ought be satisfied
Merely to live, and who, base citizen
Deprived of rights and lowliest of men,
Dares to invoke the justice of our laws!
So would it be! (act 4, scene 2).

It was especially significant that Séjour set his drama at precisely the moment when Catholic Spain, on the verge of establishing itself as a Christian nation, depended upon the non-Christian identity of Muslims and Jews to do so. In the decades between 1830 and 1860, and in response to the pressure of the abolitionist movement in the North, the antebellum South clung more fiercely to its identity as slaveholding and white. Consequently, the civil rights of the free people of color were systematically restricted, withheld, and on the eve of the Civil War, all but annulled.

Even while it draws on themes from his native land, Séjour's play also relies on staples of the nineteenth-century French theater, where dramas that featured Jewish characters or drew on biblical themes were abundant. Eugène Scribe wrote the libretto for Fromental Halévy's score of the 1835 opera, *La Juive,* the most popular of the nineteenth century.[52] Scribe and Halévy collaborated again for the 1852 opera, *Le juif errant.*[53] *L'impératrice et la juive* by A. Bourgeois appeared in 1834, and Scribe wrote *Rebecca* in 1845.[54] In 1847, the brilliant Jewish actress Rachel Félix, who revived enthusiasm for French classical drama, played the lead role in the Comédie Française's production of Racine's *Athalie.* Thematically, *The Jew of Seville* participates in both classical and popular dramatic productions of the nineteenth century; formally it is the first of only two Séjour plays written in verse. (*La Chute de Séjean,* his second play, was written in verse and was performed by the Comédie Française in 1849.)[55]

In Jean Racine's last play, *Athalie,* the young protagonist Joash is also know as Eliacin.[56] Joash must be hidden from the murderous rage of his grandmother Queen Athalie (who has already murdered everyone else in her family), just as Diégarias/Eliacin must conceal his identity to escape persecution by his in-laws. The bitter familial struggle has similar implications for Victor Séjour's Eliacin. Ultimately it is Don Juan, his wife's cousin, who destroys the Jew and his daughter. Séjour also uses themes that have their most popular expression in *The Merchant of Venice,* particularly in depicting the Jew's relationship to the Christian. Both Shylock and Diégarias are publicly disgraced by Christians who need their money; both lose their daughters to Christian men; both use their wealth to extract revenge—but here the similarities end.

Unlike Shylock, who is always the social leper, Diégarias conceals his Jewish origins and "passes" into the Christian world, where he succeeds magnificently; unlike Shylock, like a *converso* Diégarias experiences life as simultaneously an insider and an outsider. The differences are suggested by each father's response to the seduction of his daughter by a Christian. Throughout Shylock's ranting over Jessica's flight, he seems to be less wounded by her leaving than by the loss of what she took. When Tubal returns with the unhelpful news that he has not found the couple but has heard of their extravagant purchases, Shylock erupts: "Why there, there, there! A diamond gone cost me over two thousand ducats in Frankford! The curse never fell upon our nation till now; I never felt it till now. Two thousand ducats in that, and other precious, precious jewels. I would my daughter were dead at my foot, and the jewels in her ear! Would she were hearsed at my foot, and the ducats in her coffin!" (III.i.79–85 [Penguin edition, 1998]).

When Inès confesses that she has married without his consent, Diégarias already knows that the marriage is a sham but his anger is deflected by her remorse and his determination to punish Don Juan.

In a scene devoted to revelations, Inès learns the truth about her marriage from her father in this way: she tells him that she is Don Juan's wife, now the countess of Santafiel. Diégarias then looks into her eyes, and pushing her from him says in disgust: "You?... You are his concubine" (act 1, scene 7). Inès throws herself at his feet and, moved by her suffering, Diégarias takes her in his arms.

Shylock's famous discourse is a moving appeal for compassion between different peoples, but his archetypal Jewish greed is only surpassed by his hot desire for revenge; he refuses triple his original loan to watch Antonio die. Diégarias's desire for revenge is no less intense, but it is mediated by a call for justice that will only come with a revolution of the social order. Indeed when the tocsin initiates the civil war, Diégarias disrespectfully informs the king (using "tu," the second-person familiar) that he has betrayed him:

Yes, it is the people that you hear!
The sovereign people, who will persevere
Until, burning with rage, with arms of steel
Entwining you, they crush you, make you feel
Their rightful wrath, trample your crown, destroy
Your throne, whose scraps, bits, in a fit of joy,
They will refashion in a coffin for
Your royal bones!... Give ear! That mighty roar
You hear... It is the people, with one voice,
Crying out for a ruler of their choice!
Resign yourself, prince of the blood! A Jew
Has smashed the throne for all who follow you! (act 5, scene 8)

The insertion of this republican rhetoric here (completely out of place in this play) further links *The Jew of Seville* to the social and political climate back in Louisiana. In the decade before the American Civil War, it alludes to the split between the republican North and the aristocratic South where slavery, a system based on heredity, was the last vestige of the "old" world and the glaring contradiction at the heart of the Republic. Shylock wants Antonio's life and only that; Diégarias wants the end of government based on heredity, that is, the end of a social and political system based on race. Shylock remains an Outsider, but as an inside/outsider (a concept which also characterizes Séjour's Creole community) Diégarias wishes to make his revenge the catalyst for social and political revolution. Part of the reason for the erosion of the civil rights of the Creoles of color in Louisiana immediately before the Civil War was the fear that they would incite slave revolts and ultimately side with the North.

The Jew of Seville also traded on those features that made the mulatto such a popular character: exotic origins, a family secret that conceals a tragic past, an outcast with a desire for revenge.[57] Interesting too is that there were two other plays featuring a mulatto character on stage in Paris during the 1840s. Basing their work on a popular novella by Madame Reyboud, *Les Epaves,* Alexis Decomberousse and Benjamin Antier wrote *Le Marché de Saint-Pierre* in 1839, and Eugène Scribe's adaptation, *Le Code noir* appeared in 1842. It might seem a little curious that Séjour chose not to dramatize his short story "The Mulatto," but this fiery critique of plantation slavery and colonialism would never have gotten past the censors.[58] But in placing the figure of the "tragic mulatto" in Catholic/Jewish conflict, Séjour could address the way in which difference, made to look natural, is in fact socially constructed.

Even though Victor Séjour's *The Jew of Seville* seems light-years away from abolitionist texts such as William Wells Brown's *Clotel* or his own "The Mulatto," the tragic consequences for the offspring of mixed unions are the same. Moreover, the distance obtained by moving the conflict from the familiar black/Creole/white context enables Séjour's *The Jew of Seville* to make visible the *social* rather than the putative *natural* construction of *difference.* By replacing "racial" with "religious" difference Séjour dramatizes difference that is invisible, as was in fact true of many Creoles of color. For if phenotypical differences cannot be detected, how reliable a measure are they to designate categories of difference? The fear of not being able to tell who is what is the source of the obsession with designations such as "mulatto," "quadroon," and "octoroon." Nineteenth-century American social and individual identity depended on being able to see the difference between black and white, between free and slave. And although antebellum Louisiana law recognized "Creole-of-color" as separate from the designation "Negro," as the Civil War drew near, Séjour's relatively privileged community became increasingly vulnerable.

That Séjour wrote a drama set in fifteenth-century Spain that illuminates, in part, the racist practices of his native Louisiana suggests another connection. It is the poignant irony of which only history seems capable that Spain became a Catholic nation based, in part, on the "purity of blood" statutes and so expelled its Jews in the same year that Christopher Columbus discovered the "new" world—a new world that would later adapt features of those statutes to enslave and subjugate the Africans who had been brought there by force. In both content and form, Séjour's *The Jew of Seville* revisits the European origins of racist America. The African part of Séjour's ancestry was best conveyed by the pariah status of the Jew and his daughter, who like the Creoles of color were outcasts in a world that after three centuries had become their home. Now more than one hundred and fifty years later, Norman Shapiro's beautiful translation of *The Jew of Seville* will, I hope, secure Victor Séjour's place in the history of American literature.

Notes

1. Armand Lanusse, ed., *Les Cenelles: choix de poésies indigènes* (New Orleans: H. Lauvre et Compagnie, 1845).

2. T. A. Daley, "Victor Séjour," *Phylon* 4 (1943): 13; J. John Perret, "Victor Séjour, Black French Playwright from Louisiana," *French Review* 57, no. 2 (1983): 187, 192–93; James Hatch and Ted Shine, eds., *Black Theatre USA: Plays by African Americans,* vol. 1: *The Early Period, 1847–1938* (New York: Free Press, 1996).

3. Charles Barthelemy Roussève, *The Negro in Louisiana: Aspects of His History and His Literature* (1937; New York: Johnson Reprint Corporation, 1970), 77.

4. Charles Edwards O'Neill, *Séjour: Parisian Playwright from Louisiana* (Lafayette: Center for Louisiana Studies, University of Southwestern Louisiana, 1995), 153.

5. O'Neill, *Séjour,* 26, n. 24.

6. O'Neill, *Séjour,* 144, 162.

7. Bernard Peterson, *Early Black American Playwrights and Dramatic Writers* (New York: Greenwood Press, 1990), 172–75. Peterson lists *Le Vampire* as one of the unpublished plays, as does Thomas Bonner Jr. in an essay on Séjour in *The Dictionary of Literary Biography* (Thomas Bonner Jr., "Victor

Séjour," *Dictionary of Literary Biography*, ed. Trudier Harris, vol. 50 [Detroit: Gale Research Co., 1986], 237–41). Charles O'Neill, Séjour's biographer, does not. In a letter to me, Rev. O'Neill stated that he omitted *Le Vampire* from Séjour's bibliography because he was unable to locate a copy of the play in any library or archive he consulted. Neither Bonner nor Peterson includes *Henri de Lorraine,* the last play Séjour saw into production. Criticism of *Henri de Lorraine* was so severe that Séjour canceled its publication. The other unpublished play is *Cromwell,* and it too was staged in 1875.

8. Werner Sollors, *Neither Black nor White yet Both: Thematic Explorations of Interracial Literature* (New York: Oxford University Press, 1997), 164, 474 n. 6.

9. *La Tireuse de cartes* (*The Fortune-Teller*) has been translated by Norman Shapiro (Urbana: University of Illinois Press, 2002).

10. Rodolphe Lucien Desdunes, *Nos Hommes et Notre Histoire* (Montreal: Arbor et Dupont, 1911); in English, Charles Edwards O'Neill, introduction to *Our People and Our History,* by Rodolphe Lucien Desdunes (Baton Rouge: Louisiana State University Press, 1973); see also Roussève, *Negro in Louisiana.*

11. Edward Laroque Tinker, *Les Ecrits de langue française en Louisiane au XIXe siècle* (Paris: Librairie Ancienne Honoré Champion, 1932).

12. Charles Hamlin Good, "The First American Negro Literary Movement," *Opportunity* 10, no. 3 (Mar. 1932): 75–79.

13. Carl Van Vechten, "How the Theatre Is Represented in the Negro Collection at Yale," *Theatre Annual* (1943): 32–38.

14. *Creole Voices: Poems Published by Freemen of Color First Published in 1845,* ed. Edward Maceo Coleman (Washington, D.C.: Associated Publishers, 1945).

15. Victor Séjour, *Le Paletot brun* (Paris, 1859); Clive Barnes, "'Please Don't Cry' Is at Downtown Circle," *New York Times* 7 Dec. 1972: 73. Michael Feingold, "Botany? Si! Zoology? Horrors!" *Village Voice* 14 Dec. 1972: 74. The other two plays were *The Botany Lesson* by Brazilian novelist Machado de Assis and an original play by Brewster, *"Please Don't Cry and Say No."*

16. James Hatch and Ted Shine, eds., *Black Theater U.S.A: Forty-Five Plays by Black Americans, 1847–1974* (New York: Free Press, 1974). The translation is by Pat Hecht. In *Early Black Black American Playwrights and Dramatic Writers,* Peterson states that Townsend Brewster's translation is not published (174).

17. Bonner, "Victor Séjour."

18. Charles Edwards O'Neill, "Theatrical Censorship in France, 1844–1875: The Experience of Victor Séjour," *Harvard Library Bulletin* 26 (1978): 417–41.

19. Henry Louis Gates Jr. and Nellie Y. McKay, eds., *The Norton Anthology of African American Literature* (New York: W. W. Norton, 1997), 286–99. The translation is by Philip Bernard.

20. Marc Shell and Werner Sollors, eds., *The Multilingual Anthology of American Literature* (New York: New York University Press, 2000).

21. Victor Séjour, *Diégarias* (Paris, 1844). For the English translation the title has been changed to *The Jew of Seville.* All excerpts are from this edition.

22. Caryn Cossé Bell, *Revolution, Romanticism and the Afro-Creole Protest Tradition in Louisiana, 1718–1868* (Baton Rouge: Louisiana State University Press, 1997), 12–13; Roussève, *Negro in Louisiana,* 20–22, 42.

23. Bell, *Revolution, Romanticism and the Afro-Creole Protest Tradition,* 76–78.

24. Roussève, *Negro in Louisiana,* 25; Joan Martin, "Plaçage and the Louisiana Gens de Couleur Libres: How Race and Sex Defined the Lifestyles of Free Women of Color," in *Creole: The History and Legacy of Louisiana's Free People of Color,* ed. Sybil Kein (Baton Rouge: Louisiana State University Press, 2000), 57–70.

25. O'Neill, *Séjour,* 2, 5.

26. O'Neill, *Séjour,* 1–2.

27. W. E. B. Du Bois, *Black Reconstruction in America,* intro. by David Levering Lewis (1935; New York: Atheneum, 1992), 154.

28. Victor Séjour, "The Mulatto," *Revue des colonies* 3, no. 9 (Mar. 1837): 376–92.

29. John McCormick, *Popular Theatres of Nineteenth-Century France* (New York: Routledge, 1993), 6–76, 227.

30. McCormick, *Popular Theatres of Nineteenth-Century France,* 179.

31. O'Neill, *Séjour,* 45. Théophile Gautier, *Moniteur Universel* 14 July 1856: 1.

32. F. W. J. Hemmings, *The Theatre Industry in Nineteenth-Century France* (New York: Cambridge University Press, 1993), 231–35.

33. Hemmings, *Theatre Industry,* 259.

34. The actresses were banned from membership on the committee between 1850 and 1910 for reasons, besides the practice of munching sweets during the readings, that are still obscure (Hemmings, *Theatre Industry,* 258–59).

35. Hemmings, *Theatre Industry,* 258–59.

36. O'Neill, *Séjour,* 21.

37. O'Neill, *Séjour,* 24.

38. Perret, "Victor Séjour," 187–93. Théophile Gautier, *Histoire de l'art dra-*

matique en France depuis vingt-cinq ans, vol. 3 (Paris: Editions Hetzel, 1859), 237.

39. O'Neill, *Séjour,* 25, n. 20.

40. O'Neill, *Séjour,* 23–24. Review of *Diégarias* in *Revue de Paris* 57 (1844).

41. *Le Code noir: ou, Recueil des reglements rendus jusqu'à présent* (Paris: Prault, 1767; reprint, Basse-Terre and Fort-de-France: Société d'histoire de la Guadeloupe, 1980), 29–30.

42. Gates and McKay, *Norton Anthology of African American Literature.*

43. Chris Bongie, *Islands and Exiles: The Creole Identities of Post/Colonial Literature* (Stanford: Stanford University Press, 1998), 226–68. Sollors, *Neither Black nor White,* 164–65, 474 nn. 4, 5, 6.

44. Werner Sollors, "'Never Was Born': The Mulatto, an American Tragedy?" *Massachusetts Review* (Summer 1986): 296.

45. Séjour based this story on two figures from Spanish history of the period (1460–80). King Henry IV of Castile's finance minister, Diego Arias Dávila, was a converted Jew. Séjour combined the first two names, eliminating the "o" to get "Diégarias." The second figure is Diego de Susán, one of the wealthiest men of Seville. De Susán, fearing the rampage of the coming Inquisition, organized a group of fellow *conversos* to take up arms in self-defense. Legend has it that his beautiful daughter Susanna, fearful for the life of her high-born Christian lover, betrayed her father. See Harry Kamen, *The Spanish Inquisition: A Historical Revision* (New Haven: Yale University Press, 1997), 29, 46.

46. Dion Boucicault, *The Octoroon,* in *Early American Drama,* ed. Jeffrey Richards (New York: Penguin Books, 1997).

47. Kamen, *Spanish Inquisition,* 34–36, 232–42; Benzion Netanyahu, *Toward the Inquisition: Essays on Jewish and Converso History in Late Medieval Spain* (Ithaca: Cornell University Press, 1997), 76–85; James Carroll, *Constantine's Sword: The Jews and the Church* (Boston: Houghton Mifflin, 2001), 371–79.

48. Marc Shell, *Children of the Earth: Literature, Politics and Nationhood* (New York: Oxford University Press, 1993), 26–30.

49. Shell, *Children of the Earth,* 26–30.

50. *Encyclopedia Judaica,* vol. 12 (New York: Macmillan, 1971), 1022; Cecil Roth, *A History of the Marranos* (Philadelphia: Jewish Publication Society of America, 1941), 354.

51. Shell, *Children of the Earth,* 21.

52. Marie-Antoinette Allévy, *La Mise en scène en France dans la première moitié du dix-neuvième siècle* (Paris: Librairie E. Droz, 1938), 108.

53. Allévy, *Mise en scène,* 224.

54. Allévy, *Mise en scène,* 117.

55. O'Neill, *Séjour,* 29.

56. Jean Racine, *Britannicus, Phaedra, Athaliah,* trans. C. H. Sission (New York: Oxford, 1987). *Athalia* is taken from 2 Kings 2.11 and 2 Chron. 22–23.

57. Léon-François Hoffman, *Le nègre romantique* (Paris: Payot, 1973), 229.

58. Hoffman, *Nègre romantique,* 236.

The Jew of Seville

Presented for the first time in Paris, at the Théâtre-Français, July 27, 1844, with the following cast:

CHARACTERS IN THE PLAY	ACTORS	
Henri IV, king of Castile	Messrs.	Maillard
Diégarias, minister of Castile		Beauvallet
Abul-Bekri, Moorish spy		Maubant
Don Juan de Tello		Leroux
Don Sanche d'Alcora, palace officer		Randoux
The Commander		Robert
The Inquisitor		Marius
Pérez		Michaux
Don Gaétan, chamberlain		Labat
The Jailer		Mathien
Inès	Madame	Melingue
A Crier		
Grandees		

Act 1

An apartment in Diégarias's palace. It is night. A balconied window looks out on the Guadalquivir. Inès and Don Juan are on stage. Inès, seated, seems sad and musing; Don Juan, leaning against an armchair, is looking at her.

SCENE I

Don Juan, Inès

Don Juan (*to Inès*)

Come now, is something troubling you? You seem
Not like yourself. Is there some thought you deem
Unfit to share?

Inès

No, no...

Don Juan (*taking her hand*)

Then tell me, what
Weighs on your mind. Some danger?

Inès

No, none...

Don Juan

But
Why do you grow so pale? How comes it then,
Inès, that, at the very moment when,
Reveling in your love, your tenderness,
Drunken with joy, here at your feet, I bless
The heavens above that have decreed that we
Obey our hearts and let love's victory
Prevail... How comes it that, so often now,

Like a sad omen, dark thoughts cloud your brow?
Why, Inès?

Inès

Ah! Don Juan... It is the past
That keeps me prisoner. Deep remorse holds fast,
Entwines my heart...

Don Juan

Inès...

Inès

But if you need
Proof of my love, recall my traitorous deed!
Thus to betray my father! And betray
Myself no less!

Don Juan

Inès...

Inès (*interrupting him*)

No, no... I pray
You not defend my sin! For anything
You say will but compound my languishing.

Don Juan (*exaggeratedy, with a laugh*)

Come now! You sound as if you could commit
Some heinous crime!

Inès

Ah, count! What else is it
To marry thus, in secret, shamelessly?
Far better if you had permitted me
To ask my father's blessing, tell him of
Our troth, and openly confess our love.
He would have seen that you are all my life,

And would, surely, have let me be your wife,
Don Juan!

Don Juan

Not so! Despite my wealth, my youth,
My courage, and a century, in truth,
Of noble, valiant ancestors, and though
He feels a deep affection for me... No,
Never would he, a proud Diégarias,
Have listened to my plea! For though, alas,
I cannot tell you why, I know that he
Looks on my house as on an enemy.

Inès

But why? What reason?

Don Juan

How I wish I knew!
Long have I sought to learn, and still I do.

(*A brief silence*)

Inès

Ah! Worse than death, this doubt! What? Can I never
Be free of woe, but suffer thus forever?

Don Juan

Pray tell, when one is with such beauty blessed,
What can she know of woe, Inès?

Inès

You jest,
I fear!

Don Juan

Of course! Folly it is to let
Your mind such dark and deadly thoughts beget,

When all our lives are woven, through and through,
With hope and happiness! When I, when you
Ever can hold each other's loving hand,
And when you hear a tender voice command:
"Be happy!" For undone, vanquished I lie,
Ever to live your slave! No life had I
Before my eyes beheld you, you who are
Purest among all women, and so far
From this our earthly sphere—its infamies,
Its sins—that often I, on bended knees,
Feel I must flout my pride, fall at your feet,
And...

Inès

And?...

Don Juan (aside)

What am I doing?

(Aloud, quickly)

And repeat
That I am yours, Inès, with all my heart!

Inès (deeply moved)

Who was it, count, that taught you, thus, the art
To comfort me and stem my tears? Ah, yes,
It is at times like this, I must confess,
That I, weak woman that I am, gave both
My soul and very life to you in troth!

Don Juan

What happiness as well you gave me!

Inès

Oh!
Tell me again, Don Juan! Yes, tell me so

Once more! For I am happy too when thus
I see your face!...

(*Sadly again*)

Happy? Ah, woe is us!
My happiness is all too fleeting, for
Never can I forget—nay, nevermore!—
That I have wronged my father,...

Don Juan (*aside*)

Still?

Inès (*continuing*)

... that, clearly,
I must admit my sin, repent sincerely...

Don Juan (*looking out the window, pretending not to hear*)
Look! Day is dawning...

Inès

Sire...

Don Juan (*interrupting*)

Ah, noble sight!
Is not Seville, Inès, a sheer delight?
A city like no other?

Inès

Yes, but...

Don Juan (*likewise*)

See
How splendidly it shines, how brilliantly...

Inès
Yes, quite...

Don Juan (*likewise*)

And how your palace walls appear,
There, by the banks of the Guadalquivir,
To rival with the very Alcazar
In sumptuous grace!

Inès

I care not how they are!
What matters it to me, whose only thought
Is to repair the ill my sin has wrought,
Whose only wish is to repent, restore
Quickly the honor that was mine before,
And, once more, pay heed to a daughter's duty!
What care I if Seville, in all its beauty,
Shines bright! If the Guadalquivir rolls on
And on, relentlessly, ever anon!
Or if my palace, as you say, outvies
The king's in elegance, and charms our eyes!
What matters it to me?... My soul is much
Too filled with terror to be moved by such
Delights!... Ah, count! I fear that others will
Denounce me to my father for the ill
That I have done him, all for love of you!

Don Juan

Fear not. We have done all that we could do,
And taken every wise precaution.

Inès

Yes,

But...

Don Juan

Listen...

Inès

I...

Don Juan

Listen to me, Inès.
I know the pain, the torment you endure—
You above all, so innocent, so pure
Of heart—to keep a secret that must be
So hurtful to your pride, your modesty.
I know... But please, you must! I beg you not
To flinch in your resolve, else will our lot—
Should you reveal it—pay a frightful cost,
And everything we have... all will be lost,
In but a moment, gone!

Inès

Alas!... Ah, count!
If what you say is true, I must surmount
My fear and do your will until the end!
I only pray your stalwart hand defend
And succor me!

Don Juan

Look, it grows light... Adieu!

Inès

What? Must you go?

Don Juan (*throwing his cape over his arm*)

Until night falls anew...
Farewell!

Inès (*holding him back*)

Wait!

Don Juan

What is it?

Inès

Your sword?

Don Juan (*placing it in his belt*)

Ah! Right!

Inès (*clinging to him*)

Alas! To live without you till tonight!

Don Juan (*embracing her*)

I love you! Think of me!

(*He steps out the window onto the balcony, to which is attached a silken rope ladder.*)

Inès (*grasping his hand*)

May heaven consent
To guide you safely, without incident.

(*Don Juan disappears down the rope. Leaning out the window, Inès watches his descent.*)

SCENE 2

Inès (*alone*)

There!... He embarks... And now, godspeed, my love!
Off... Off he goes...

(*Coming downstage, sadly*)

Alas, good God above,
Now is he gone! How empty is it here!

(*She sits down.*)

How cold this place! Don Juan was right, I fear,
To find me sad and somber! Ah, the wrenching
Pain in my heart! The smart, the clenching
Anguish I feel! It is a sign, I know,
An omen of some dire, impending woe!
Oh, how these four walls stifle me!

(*Looking heavenward*)

How I
Wish I could spread a veil across the sky—
Would God but grant a faëry's art to me—
And cloak its brilliance in obscurity!

(*Musing sadly*)

Alone... Ever alone...

(*Diégarias enters, unseen by Inès, and approaches her.*)

SCENE 3
Diégarias, Inès, then Pérez

Diégarias

Inès?

Inès (*seeing him, getting up*)

Good-day,
Father.

Diégarias

You seem absorbed in thought. What may
The matter be?

Inès

The matter? Nothing...

Diégarias

Some
Dark mystery?

Inès

I saw you not, sire. Come,
Sit here by me.

Diégarias

Not now...

Inès

Oh? Why?

Diégarias

I must
Be off at once.

Inès

Whereto?

Diégarias

To our august
Majesty's court.

Inès

Your Excellency, thus,
Has matters of great import to discuss?
The realm...?

Diégarias (*gravely*)
Perhaps...

(*Pérez enters.*)

Pérez (*to Diégarias, pointing to the wings*)
Abul-Bekri, señor!

Diégarias
Good! I await him. Show him in.

(*During the preceding, Inès has taken an empty vase from a flower-laden table, and moves to leave. Diégarias addresses her.*)

Wherefore
Would you go out, Inès, at such an hour?

Inès
Merely to spend a moment in the flower
Garden, and then return at once.

(*She exits as Abul-Bekri enters.*)

SCENE 4
Diégarias, Abul-Bekri

Diégarias (*seeing Abul-Bekri*)
Aha!
Abul-Bekri! Come in, come in!

Abul-Bekri (*bowing*)
Allah
Protect you!

Diégarias (*approaching him*)
Well?

Abul-Bekri
I have the proof.

Diégarias
Where?

Abul-Bekri (*handing him a parchment*)
Here!

Diégarias (*seizing it, reading*)
"To Don Guzmán de Castro, cavalier..."

(*Muttering*)

Yes, yes... Et cetera... Let me read on...

(*Reading*)

"About to seize the crown..."

(*Aside*)

Ha!

(*Reading*)

"Don
Alphonse counts more than ever on the true
Devotion of the soldiers sworn to you.
May they be equal to the task! This night
Shall you set out, to reach Seville when bright
The noonday sky, without the walls. For we
Shall strike our blow tomorrow, when we three—
Don Luc, Don Pedro, and myself no less—
Are hunting with the king. Now can you guess?
While thus he is indulging in his bold
Heroics, we three will surround him, hold
Him fast, take prisoner His Majesty,
And turn the palace to a nunnery!..."

Abul-Bekri (*laughing*)
Enthusiasm makes us just a whit
Less than discreet!

Diégarias (*finishing the letter*)
"Adieu... Don Juan..."

(*Examining the parchment*)

But it

Says nothing of Don Sanche. Why? How is there
No mention of his name?

Abul-Bekri

We know not where
The blackguard is, señor. He covers up
His tracks too well.

Diégarias

And he, impudent pup,
Is whom we have to fear the most! Not for
His craftiness as a conspirator,
Or for his artful wiles and utter skill,
But for that sheer, indomitable will
Of his!

(*Brandishing the parchment*)

Well, never mind! I have them now!

(*After rereading to himself*)

Ah! Precious, precious letter!

(*To Abul-Bekri*)

Tell me, how
Come you to have it?

Abul-Bekri

How? I won it.

Diégarias

"Won"?

Abul-Bekri

Well, so to speak!

Diégarias

And from what mother's son?

Abul-Bekri

Fernand.

Diégarias

The servant of Don Juan?

Abul-Bekri

The very

One!

Diégarias

Did he take you for some adversary?
Some vile inquisitor?

Abul-Bekri

No.

Diégarias

But, unless
I err, he is reputed to possess
Great courage, that one! You yourself have said
That he is incorruptible, well-bred
In honor and fidelity.

Abul-Bekri

He was.

Diégarias

He "was"? What do you mean? Why "was"?

Abul-Bekri

Because,
As I once said, he would have rather died

Than breach the trust his master would confide
In him, or breathe a confidence.

Diégarias

Dead?

Abul-Bekri

Quite!

At times, to satisfy our appetite
For proof of this or that, we must, perforce,
Despite our tender feelings, have recourse
To stringent measures.

Diégarias

Horrors!

Abul-Bekri

I agree.

But surely, señor, better him than me!

Diégarias

True... So, explain what happened, if you will.
Every detail.

Abul-Bekri (*wryly*)

The city of Seville,

As you well know, is a magnificent
And lovely place, where every resident
Sleeps a sleep sound and deep! So sound, in fact,
That when, perchance, someone is robbed, attacked,
Killed even, he can be interred at some
Corner, with no fear that the law will come
Disturb the peace!

Diégarias

Indeed...

Abul-Bekri

And, doubtless, you
Know that the warders would have much to do—
More than one might expect them to, I fear!—
Were they to chase each midnight cavalier
Seeking adventure!

Diégarias

True, true...

Abul-Bekri

Well, our friend,
Fernand, came thus to his untimely end;
I saw him lurking by some hovel wall.
He sees me, suddenly. "Stop! Stop!" I call,
Standing before him. And he stops. "Give me
The message, or prepare never to see
Another dawning day!" At first he tries
To pass... In vain... Then does he realize
That he has little choice, and draws his sword...
Lunges... Only to plunge to his reward,
For, in a trice, with but a single blow,
Bloodied, my scimitar has laid him low.

Diégarias
Thank you. Now go!

Abul-Bekri

Excuse the indiscretion,
Señor... A word...

(*Reaching under his cape*)

Something in my possession
Will you find of great interest, and worth
Your time. You know that slime, scum of the earth,
Don Juan de Tello...

Diégarias

So?

Abul-Bekri

So, learn how vile
The lecher is, how base, how full of guile,
As this will show.

(*He pulls out a letter.*)

Diégarias

Another letter?

Abul-Bekri

Yes.
To Don Ruy. Listen.

(*Reading*)

"With great distress
I must refuse the loan you ask of me.
Not so much as one thin maravedi
Have I, dear friend!"

(*Speaking*)

Lies! Lies!

(*Looking at the letter, addressing it*)

Don Juan, you lie!

(*Continuing to read*)

"Poor as a churchmouse, as they say, am I!"

(*Speaking*)

He lies like some foul Jew!

Diégarias (*with a sudden shudder*)
What?

Abul-Bekri (*with a knowing smile*)
Nothing...

(*Continuing to read*)

"Yet
More is there now to tell, for I must let
You know the wager that, one night, we made—
During an orgiastic escapade,
The Duc de Lerme and I—a wager so
Monstrous, that, should we die tonight, I know
That closed to us, shut tight, would be the gates
Of that sweet paradise, where God awaits
With music pure, and of the holiest."

(*Speaking, to Diégarias*)

Just between us, I think one might suggest
That such a vicious rake might well find more
Comfort with *our* god—yours and mine, señor!

Diégarias (*motioning him to continue*)

Read on!

Abul-Bekri
Indeed... Here is the wager that
It pleased our reprobate aristocrat
To make:

(*Reading*)

"Whichever, in one month, engages
In the most senseless duels; whichever wages
A life more dissolute; whichever will
Seduce more wenches and, with the more skill,
Conquer their hearts, he shall the victor be,
And win two thousand ducats!"

Diégarias

Misery me!
What villainy! To think that God above
Could make such whoresons the descendants of
El Cid Campeador!

Abul-Bekri (*aside*)

Ha! If he knew
How much worse I, for such a sum, would do!

Diégarias (*gesturing*)
Go on!

Abul-Bekri (*continuing to read*)
"The duke, as you might have expected,
Undertook his endeavor, and neglected
Never a single opportunity
To ply his villainous debauchery.
Myself, I found it not so simple: I
Happened, straightway, upon a radiant, shy,
Pink maid of eighteen years, pure as a star
That lights the morning sky, sparkling afar
But with a heart unyielding to my pleading
Without a proper marriage. Thus, proceeding,
One dark night, to my chapel, secretly,
Not without many an obstacle, were we
Soon joined in holy wedlock by..."

(*To Diégarias*)

By?... Guess!...

By?...

(*Reading*)

"By Fernand!..."

Diégarias (*seizing the letter from him*)

Fernand? His servant? Bless

My soul!

Abul-Bekri (*stifling a laugh*)

How judge you, then, this confidence,

Señor?

Diégarias (*angrily*)

How?

(*Throwing a purse at him, scornfully*)

That you earned your recompense,

Scoundrel!

Abul-Bekri (*vexed, aside*)

Not yet!

A Page (*entering, announcing*)

The king!

A Second Page (*likewise*)

His Majesty!

(*The King, dressed in a hunting costume, enters as Abul-Bekri and the two pages exit.*)

SCENE 5

The King, Diégarias, then Inès

Diégarias (*bowing down*)
Most honored is your servant, sire, to be
Graced with your royal presence.

(*He rises.*)

The King (*casually*)
Oh... I say...

Diégarias
I was, in truth, myself, about to pay
A visit to the court. Matters of state...

The King
I see...

Diégarias
Problems, concerns...

The King
Yes... They can wait,
Diégarias! Indeed, I have not come
For that!... Now...

(*Writing*)

"For His Majesty, the sum
Of six hundred doubloons..."

(*Stopping*)

I must admit,
The sum is rather high for but a bit
Of finery! But, for a king, what matters

Money! Doña Quiomar desires! It flatters
Her pride. And she shall have it!

(*He signs the note and gives it to Diégarias.*)
Here!

Diégarias (*aside*)
Again?

The King
Be quick!

Diégarias
Sire… If His Majesty would deign
Give me a moment…

The King
Now! Time presses…

Diégarias
But
Of the most grievous urgency is what
I have to say!

The King
Later! The money, please!
Without delay!

Diégarias
Duty, I fear, decrees…

The King
That you obey!

Diégarias (*continuing*)
… that I inform you, sire,
However much I might incur your ire

And run the risk of punishment, that we
Have precious little in the treasury.

The King (*somewhat taken aback*)
Perhaps...

Diégarias (*continuing*)
And that your people take a dim
View of more taxes at the royal whim!

The King
True...

Diégarias (*continuing*)
That the army still awaits its pay
For five months now!

The King (*arms crossed, half serious, half in jest, laughing*)
Indeed! No doubt!... I say,
You seem about to let your passion for
The public good well up in you once more,
And carry you away! Must you, again,
As is your fashion, criticize my reign
And lecture me, spreading before my eyes
My subjects' woeful state, my grandees' lies,
Deceits, their plots, their infamies, and all
That dismal, dark, unholy folderol
Of frightful thoughts, dismaying doubts, fears—some
Quite senseless!—that makes any king succumb
And turn his throne into the wrack!... Ah, no!

(*Becoming more serious*)

Speak of the loving zephyrs that will blow
And lull the lazy barque. Speak of the joys
And pleasures of the hunt, with all its noise,
Its danger; of the forest, of the skies,

The orange groves, where, leisurely, one lies
Listening to his heart, sighing his sighs,
Free of the weighty scepter, and without
An empire's burden...

Diégarias (*gravely*)

You are king.

The King

No doubt...
And if the morrow were to float, perchance,
Our flag above the battlefield's expanse,
Then, underneath our banner, raised aloft,
Baring our sword that, many a time and oft,
Dripped with Granada's blood, would we declare
To our staunch soldiers massing there: "Prepare!
The danger grows! But it is only right
That I, your king, should be the first to fight!"

(*Laughing*)

Ha!... But for now I abdicate! No taste
Have I but for the hunt, and must make haste,
For too much time already waste I here
In idle talk! So, trusty financier,
Let me go off, or come join me therein,
Blade in one hand, Diégarias, and in
The other, my doubloons! Come...

(*He goes to leave.*)

Diégarias (*standing in his way*)

No, wait! Please,
Listen and save your life! No more are these
Mere threats, mere rumors, intrigues come to naught!
It is a trap, and you, sire, shall be caught
In it today!

The King

Today?

Diégarias

This very day
Are they about to strike, I tell you!

The King

"They"...?

Diégarias

During the hunt, it is their plan to make
Their move, to seize Your Majesty and take
Him prisoner.

The King

Seize me? Seize me? Who would dare?
Who?

Diégarias

Those who shrink from nothing, sire, in their
Villainies! Here, see for yourself.

(*He hands him the letter.*)

The King (*after reading it*)

Damn!

(*Crumpling it, angrily*)

Damn!
How can they envy me? King though I am,
I cannot leave my prison, venture out,
But that conspiracies begin to sprout
Beneath my feet! Plots, intrigues, treachery...

(*He pauses.*)

Diégarias

Already have I warned Your Majesty—
Perhaps too frankly, sire, though not mistaken
Was I—that soon the empire, rudely shaken
To its foundations, would no doubt be faced
With a disaster; that some highly placed
Nobles, grandees, subjects drunken with power
Were busy plotting many an evil hour
For you! That, if you did not wish to see
Greater and greater the ignominy
Of their behavior, or see them, in time,
Rise to the pinnacle of violent crime,
It well behooved you, in the harshest wise,
To lay them low, with neither compromise
Nor mercy, sire, and cast in chains their base
Disloyalty! Then could you move apace,
Peacefully, with no fear that you would light
The angry flames of discord, or ignite
A civil war. Then could you have cut out
The poison at its source, hewn down—without
Leaving a trace—the tree of treachery!
And still you may... But if you disagree,
Disdain my words, and treat with pity those
Daft, deranged felons, then you may suppose
That, overnight, the state, thanks to the blow
They strike, will cease to be the state we know.

The King (*bursting out suddenly*)

No! I refuse! Good God, I have not reckoned
My days to be another Juan the Second,
Poor predecessor weak of will, and all
My reign to languish piteously in thrall!

(*Pacing back and forth*)

What profits me to be the master! Me,
The king! I who, alas, am never free

Of fear, of doubt, imprisoned day and night
In my abode, ever aghast with fright
Lest, should I dare go out, wrench myself from
The safety of my throne, I might become
The victim of some hidden blade!... Ah! I
Have had enough! Enough! What? They would try
To fill my life with terror, tears, despair?
So be it then! But here and now I swear
That they will pay a price for every tear
That they have made me shed! A price most dear
In blood!

(*He takes a quill and begins to sign an arrest decree, but stops suddenly, sighing.*)

Ah...

(*Reflecting, sadly*)

Blood...

(*There is a moment of silence.*)

Diégarias

Have you some stratagem
That stays your hand, sire?

The King

None...

(*Throwing down the quill*)

I pardon them.

Diégarias (*surprised*)

Pardon...? Your Majesty, I fear that most unwise
Is such a course! Indeed, you jeopardize

The power of the crown if they not be
Punished for such a foul conspiracy!
Some will surmise—

The King (*interrupting*)

I have decided.

Diégarias

Sire...

The King

No! I have spoken! And though dread and dire
May be the harm to kingly power when one
Shows too much kindness, and though I, undone
By my own will, refusing thus to bring
Traitors to justice, still am I a king
Who takes no pleasure in the punishing
Of such as flout his strength and break his laws.
What can I do? My nature is the cause:
My heart is barren of bloodthirstiness
And violent, murderous thoughts, and I confess,
A weak king would I choose to be, far more
Than those whose scepters reek of blood and gore.

Diégarias

But weak ones, as you doubtless have heard said,
When blows the tempest, lose both crown and head!

The King

And die content!

Diégarias

But not without remorse
For having sown the seeds, and been the source,
Of death, corruption, civil strifes, hates, woes,
And base ambition, in a land where those

Who had looked to their king to bring them peace,
Happy tranquillity, and a surcease
From life's travail, know bitterness and pain.

(*At that moment Inès enters, unseen by the others, carrying a vase full of flowers. She stops short, listening.*)

The King
True...

(*With disgust*)

But, for these foul curs, I say again,
Whatever punishment my law demands,
I will not, right or wrong, allow my hands
To wallow in three victims' blood!

Diégarias

But sire,
I merely said that those who thus conspire
Against Your Majesty must be chastised,
And vigorously. But I never advised
Punishment dire in the extreme. No, truly,
I deem one sentence, executed duly,
Will quite suffice. Let one of these vile three
Be put to death, and calm, I guarantee,
Will be restored, and peace will reign, with ample
Benefit from this one most base example.

The King
And which one then?

Diégarias

The one who, for a third
Time now, defying you, your wrath, has erred...
Erred?... Sinned, Your Majesty!...

The King

Ah? And which one

Would that one be, Diégarias?

Diégarias

Don Juan.

Inès (*alarmed, choking back a whisper*)

Good God! Don Juan...

The King (*after a pause*)

Ah yes... I wonder how
His treasons, hatred, pride have not, by now,
Cured me of that unthinking, childish fear
Of mine, that makes me shrink before a mere
Trickle of blood!... Well, be that as it may,
I must be off, betake myself away
From your advice and influence, to muse
Upon his crime, and how best I may choose
To wreak my vengeance. Till tomorrow...

(*As Diégarias is about to object, authoritatively*)

Till

Tomorrow!

(*Calling into the wings, as Diégarias bows*)

Don Sanche!

Don Sanche (*appearing at the door, upstage, to The King*)

Sire? Your pleasure?

The King (*to Don Sanche*)

Will

You go announce that we wish to abate
The hunt!

Don Sanche

Yes, sire.

(*Aside*)

Damn! We shall have to wait
And try again!

(*He leaves.*)

The King (*to Diégarias*)

There!

(*Holding out his hand for him to kiss*)

Are you satisfied,
My friend?

(*Turning to leave*)

Adieu. Much have I to decide.

(*He leaves.*)

Diégarias (*following him out*)

Sire...

(*As he leaves, Inès comes out of hiding.*)

SCENE 6

Inès (*alone*)

Oh! My head... My mind... What did I hear?
Don Juan... Die?... No, it cannot be! My ear
Deceives me!

(*Noticing that Diégarias is about to return*)

Ah! My father!... God, I pray
You succor me! Tell me what words to say
To move his heart!

SCENE 7
Inès, Diégarias

Diégarias (*entering, to Inès*)
So, you return, I see.

Inès
Yes, father.

(*Forcing a smile*)

Not too soon, I trust...

Diégarias
For me,
How could it be too soon? You, who see clearly
Into my heart, who see me burdened, nearly
Bowed low with age; who know how much you render
My voyage calm and sweet... You, angel tender,
Do you know how I love you?

(*He embraces her.*)

Inès
Yes, I do...
But... Tell me... When the king was here with you,
Conversing... If, by some rare circumstance,
Not knowing he was here... If... If, perchance,
I had arrived and heard, by accident,
Word of some grave, hateful predicament...
If I had learned about some... Something... Some
Secret... What would you do?

Diégarias (*smiling*)

I would become
Terrified, frankly, overcome with fright
To think that any secret of mine might
Fall on a woman's ears! And you? What would
You do?

Inès

Me?

Diégarias (*with a laugh*)

You.

Inès

Alas!

(*Resolutely*)

I think I should
Tell you the truth, and not embellish it,
Or hide it from you.

Diégarias

What?

Inès

I must admit,
Father, that I was here...

(*Pointing to where she had been standing, unseen*)

There.

Diégarias

You were...

Inès

Yes...

I heard...

Diégarias

But...

Inès

Oh! Would that more tenderness
Could move you! Would that you were less severe,
Less harsh, father!

Diégarias

Inès...

Inès

It would appear
That you were asking that His Majesty
Should put to death some noble, some grandee...
Somebody named Don Juan, unless I much
Mistake...

Diégarias

True.

Inès

But what crime is his for such
A fate?

Diégarias

He has conspired.

Inès

Against you, sire?

Diégarias

No, not against myself. His is a higher,
More vicious crime.

Inès

Against the state?

Diégarias

Indeed.

Inès (*aside*)

Help me, dear God!

(*Aloud*)

I know it is decreed
By law that such a great and grave offense
Call down upon his head a recompense
Austere and swift, and that the scaffold, at the very
Least, be the price such revolutionary
Felons must pay. But if the king, who is
The most aggrieved by this base deed of his,
Relents, loath to wreak vengeance on this young
And thoughtless miscreant, why must your tongue
Continue to demand—you, sire, so kind
Of heart—that what the king is ill inclined
To do, be done? Tell me...

Diégarias

His interest
Requires it.

Inès

Ah! But, surely, he knows best!
A king who lets his mercy rule his hand
Is far more loved—revered!—throughout his land

Than one who chooses to be feared! Pray, please
Let him follow his heart at times like these.

Diégarias

"At times like these..." Yes, child, I fear you see
Only the present clearly. As for me,
I see the future.

Inès

But a future bought
With blood bodes ill!

Diégarias

Some heinous crimes one ought
Be quick to punish.

Inès

Yes, but have you no
Qualms that, when, like yourself, one has been so
Compassionate, it may be thought by those
Who envy you, and who wish to dispose
Others against you, that your obstinate
Inclemency is the result of hate
And enmity?

Diégarias

What do I care for them,
As long as you, Inès, do not condemn
Your father for his deed, but realize
That Castile spreads, proudly, before his eyes
When, cruel, his hand strikes its fell blow!

Inès

And who
Assures you, father, that my own heart too
Does not give way to bitter doubts when thus
I see you so unbending, murderous!

Diégarias

Please, speak not so, Inès.

Inès

Mad I may be,
But I await your words to comfort me;
To tell me, sire... To swear that it is not
Hatred of him that drives you on.

Diégarias (*after a weighty silence, sighing*)

Ah...

Inès

What?
You hesitate?

Diégarias

That will I never swear!
I cannot! Not with all the scorn I bear
From him and his accursèd race! My brow
Wears deep their infamy! No, let me now
Hate them and him, and hate my fill!

Inès

What? Scorn?
You, who, of every noble Spaniard born,
Are the most honored? You, risen so far
Above your humble birth? You, once a mere
Adventurer, who so much could endear
Your person to His Majesty, that he
Entrusts to you the Royal Treasury!
What scorn is this?

Diégarias

My child, you speak the truth.
But if the secret of my past, my youth,
Were known tomorrow in his state, in this

City that I pull from the precipice
Of civil war... If my face should reveal
The dread, the apprehension that I feel,
And were someone to spy it, and to fling
My forebears' name before the court, the king,
Then would you see my power crumble, my
Name, now so honored, lauded, by and by
Become a curse, a blasphemy! And all
My climb would be but prelude to my fall.
This is the truth; I know whereof I speak.

Inès

But... What dark secret is it? What could wreak
Such woe?

Diégarias

For fifteen years my life has been
Veiled in deceit...

Inès

Go on...

Diégarias

Yes, now I mean
To tell you all, with no regret, for you
Surely will not denounce me to those who
Would wish me ill.

Inès

Good God!

Diégarias (*looking around to make sure no one else is listening*)

My child, give ear!

Inès

What frightful thing am I about to hear,
Father?

Diégarias

For years, Castile, Spain, everyone—
All of my friends, and you above all—none
Was there but would assume that I, like you...
You, Christian heart and soul... that I, I too,
Must be the same. But though you would believe
What passed for truth, beliefs, alas, deceive.
For I am not.

Inès (softly)

Not Christian, father? Why?
What are you then? If my God you deny,
What God is yours? Whose do you worship? Whose
Faith do you follow?

Diégarias

I will not abuse
You longer, child. My griefs, my misery
Shall give the answer! Let them speak for me.

Inès

Heavens!

Diégarias

I was a youth of twenty years—
An age when there is nothing that appears
Impossible!—and though my birth was base,
And I a pauper, still, the noble race,
The wealth, the proud escutcheon of a fair,
Glorious maiden tempted me, and there
I was, in love with her! Bianca was she,
Your mother, child. Each evening, faithfully,

Would she go to the convent, there to spend
An hour in fervent prayer. And I would wend
My way there too, watching her pray—sad, mute...
When she would leave, my eyes, quick in pursuit,
Would follow her... One morning, though, I had
A letter from her uncle, who forbade
Me—for he had discerned my love—to try
To speak to her!... I, who would gladly die
Merely to look upon her face!... For not
Was I her equal!

Inès

And...?

Diégarias

And not a jot
Did I pay heed!

Inès

And then?

Diégarias

And then... Then... Oh!
The shame! The infamy!

Inès

What? Tell me...

Diégarias

Woe
Is me! Ah, woe is me!... He had his men
Drag me within his palace walls. And then...

Inès

God!

Diégarias

How the thought still galls my soul!... They bound
Me, hand and foot, held fast, and, to compound
The villainy, as if I were some wretch,
Some cur, he promptly sent them round to fetch
Two lackeys, shaking sticks, laughing to see
Me quake with fright as they came after me...

Inès

No!

Diégarias

Then he gave the order.

Inès

What? You mean...

Diégarias (*convulsed with sarcasm*)

My child, such has Castilian vengeance been
For me and mine! After all, could one think
That he, a fine grandee, would dare to sink
So low... He, of a proud nobility,
Whose ancient and sublime family tree
Goes back to Charlemagne, or Caesar's Gaul...
No, no... Could one suppose that, after all,
He could dare sink so low that he would show
Respect for such as me... Treat me as though
I were a man... A citizen?... No! Why?
Because I was a Jew!

Inès

A Jew?

Diégarias (*growing more and more enraged*)

Yes! I
Was one of those they kick aside, those whom

They name with utter scorn, those whom they doom—
And with impunity!—to be dragged off,
Off to their palace, where two lackeys scoff
And laugh as they stand beating you! A Jew,
Inès!

Inès (*trying to calm him*)
Please, father! Please!...

Diégarias (*after a pause, continuing*)
When they were through,
When I had been disgraced, shamed more than one
Should have to bear, no feelings had I, none,
Save rage, and loathing, and a wounded pride.
With but one thought lurking about inside
My soul, by day and night: to seize him—that
Unholy, murderous aristocrat—
Who, in one bloody hour, had rent asunder
My life... To press him, gasping, panting, under
My dagger's doughty steel!...

(*Sighing*)

I am afraid
That hour aged me a hundred years, and made
A ruthless judge out of a simple lad.

Inès
What of my mother, sire?

Diégarias
Your mother had
Only one wish: "Come, let us flee!" said she.
Heartsore, yet still was I quick to agree,
For love held sway over my bitterness.
And so we fled. Greece it was that would bless

Us with her welcome. There, calm and content,
Confident in our happiness, I went
From poverty to wealth, and soon became
A man much honored. But in vain! My shame
Lived yet within me, flourished, thrived, beset
My heart, my mind... For I could not forget
That vile offense!... At length, Inès, your mother
Died...

Inès (*sighing*)
Ah...

Diégarias
And, in my arms, left me no other
Parting request but that I do my best,
One day, to bring her ashes here. No rest
Knew I: that wish was my command. But first,
Still diffident, and fearful of the worst,
I took another name, and then returned,
Hiding my faith so well that no one learned,
After my twenty years in exile spent,
That this grandee—proud, wealthy, eminent
Diégarias—had, in truth, ever been
The lowly Jew, Jacob Eliacin!

Inès
Ah! But—

Diégarias (*interrupting, sarcastically*)
And if, perhaps, you wish to hear
The name of that fine, noble cavalier,
Listen, Inès! Listen, and mark it well:
Don Diegue de Tello, count of Santafiel!

Inès (*shocked*)
The father of Don Juan?

Diégarias

No other, child!
Oh, what delight he took! He smirked, he smiled,
He laughed to see his vulgar lackeys set
Upon me, torturing my soul... And yet,
To think he died without repaying me
His debt of infamous indignity!
Ah, but I have not fed my wrath for naught!
The son shall pay for what the father wrought!

Inès

Oh! Mercy, father! Mercy!

Diégarias

He shall die!
Why should I hide the truth? Why should I lie
And say that he shall not!

Inès (*desperately*)

Don Juan?... No! No!
Not him! Upon your soul, I beg you show
Compassion, sire! For me!... Pray, spare his life!

Diégarias

For you? Why... Why for you?

Inès (*throwing herself at his feet, softly*)

I am his wife.

Diégarias

His... No! That cannot be!

(*Raising her*)

This is a joke,
Inès... I know. You wish but to provoke
Me, shock me... Tell me so.

Inès (*struggling with her emotions*)
I cannot, sire.
I am countess of Santafiel.

Diégarias (*glaring at her*)
No! Liar!...
You mean... You mean you are his concubine!
His loathsome mistress...

(*Pushing her away, disdainfully*)

But no daughter mine!

Inès (*with dignity*)
I blush with shame to hear such an offense,
So undeserved, flung at my innocence.
No, love it was that bound us—pure, sincere:
I am his wife, and not his mistress.

(*There is a pause while Diégarias reflects.*)

Diégarias (*handing her Don Juan's letter*)
Here,
Read this, I pray.

Inès
This?... What? A letter? Who...

(*As she reads it to herself*)

O God! No!... O, my God! It is not true!

(*She takes her head in her hands, sobbing.*)

Diégarias (*deeply moved, taking her hand*)
Be strong! Such sorrow will, in time, be healed.

Inès (*about to throw herself at his feet, contritely*)
Father...

Diégarias (*stopping her, taking her in his arms*)
No... Come, my child...

(*As they stand, embracing, aside, with determination*)

His fate is sealed!

CURTAIN

Act 2

Same scene as in act I

SCENE I
Diégarias, Abul-Bekri

Diégarias (*to Abul-Bekri*)
What is the hour?

Abul-Bekri
Midnight approaches.

Diégarias
Come...

(Pointing to a purse on the table)

There is my purse. Take it.

(*Abul-Bekri complies, passing the purse from hand to hand.*)

What is the sum?

Abul-Bekri
A tidy one, I warrant, by the weight!

Diégarias
How much?

(*Abul-Bekri takes out the coins and sets them in a pile, gazing at them.*)

Abul-Bekri (*aside*)
Damnation!

(*Aloud, to Diégarias*)

I would estimate...

Diégarias
Exactly, please.

Abul-Bekri (*counting*)
Six score doubloons, señor.

Diégarias
Quite so, Abul-Bekri. A goodly store,
Would you agree?

Abul-Bekri (*smiling*)
Would I...? Why, just last year,
A friend of mine and I were chatting here,
And I, señor... Said I to him, for such
A sum as that there was not very much
I would not do!

Diégarias
Good! And you think so still?

Abul-Bekri
Oh, I...

Diégarias
You would not change your mind?

Abul-Bekri
That will
Depend...

Diégarias
On?

Abul-Bekri

Well…

Diégarias (*insisting*)

Tell me! You would not change
Your mind?

Abul-Bekri (*after looking at him intently*)

No.

Diégarias

Good! Then, if I should arrange
To take revenge for a vile infamy,
I could depend on you, Abul-Bekri?

Abul-Bekri

Yes.

Diégarias

On your blade as well?

Abul-Bekri

Yes.

Diégarias

And you would—

Abul-Bekri (*interrupting*)

Obey, señor!

Diégarias

Ah! Even if it should
Mean that a loathsome man must die?

Abul-Bekri

Then I
Shall kill him.

Diégarias

Without mercy?

Abul-Bekri

Let him ply
Me with his tears, señor, and cry, and weep!
A deaf ear shall I turn!

Diégarias

And you will keep
Your word? You swear?

Abul-Bekri

Rest easy! You can be
Sure!

Diégarias

And the weapon you will use? Show me.
Where is it?

Abul-Bekri (*opening his cape*)

Here.

Diégarias

Then we agree. Good!... So...

(*Pointing to the door, stage left*)

Into this chamber straightway will you go,
Quietly, making not a sound!... Soon—

Abul-Bekri (*interrupting*)

Yes,
I know, señor! Whoever—Diegue, López,
Whatever be his name—grandee, bourgeois,
Knight of Santiago, of Alcantara,

Whoever... You have but to say the word,
And it is done.

Diégarias

Ah...

Abul-Bekri

Nothing shall be heard
From him again!

Diégarias

So be it!

Abul-Bekri (*with a bow, taking the purse*)

Master...

Diégarias (*seizing his arm*)

Just
One moment!

Abul-Bekri

My doubloons...

Diégarias

No! First you must
Earn them!

Abul-Bekri (*putting down the purse*)

Indeed! And so I shall!

(*Aside*)

If he
Knew what a secret I possess, then we
Might see him act with more respect!

(*With an obsequious nod*)

Señor...

(*Aside*)

That would he pay to still my tongue... and more!

(*He pauses.*)

Diégarias
What are you waiting for?

(*Pointing to the door*)

Go! It is time!

Abul-Bekri (*bowing*)
Master!

(*Aside*)

My time will come!

(*He leaves.*)

SCENE 2

Diégarias (alone)
God! To what crime
Am I reduced! What dark demands havc made
Me stoop to such a deed!

(*Pérez enters, carrying a sword.*)

SCENE 3
Diégarias, Pérez

Pérez (*holding out the sword to Diégarias*).

Señor, his blade...

Diégarias

Give it to me!

(*Putting it in his belt, whispering*)

So! Are your orders clear?

Pérez (*whispering*)

Yes, master.

(*Pointing to the window, stage right*)

I shall hide myself out here,
Beneath the window. Someone will arrive...
A man... He will climb up... If, still alive,
He climbs down, then, one word from you, señor,
And I shall kill him, dead.

Diégarias

Indeed!... No more
Need you delay.

(*Gesturing*)

Be off!

(*Pérez leaves. Diégarias, attaching the rope ladder to the window, continues, apostrophizing.*)

Ah, by and by,
Shall you come meet your doom!

(Reading from Don Juan's letter)

"... a radiant, shy,
Pink maid of eighteen years, pure as a star
That lights the morning sky, sparkling afar..."

(*After perusing the rest of the letter in silence*)

He mentions not her name. So much the better!
No one need ever know!

(*Brandishing it*)

O cursèd letter!
Let him resist, and die he shall! Then he
Will take the secret to eternity!

(*Three handclaps are heard from outside.*)

Ah! Him!... Now let him come!

(*Throwing down the ladder*)

This is for you,
Don Juan, lest you not keep your rendezvous!

(*He hides behind the curtains. Don Juan appears at the top of the ladder.*)

SCENE 4

Don Juan, Diégarias, then Abul-Bekri

Don Juan (*propping himself on the sill, obviously encumbered, aside*)
A little too much wine... Perhaps with less
Baggage to weigh me down...

(*He takes off his cape and flings it inside, onto the floor. Removing his sword, aloud*)

My sword, Inès...
Here, take it...

(*Diégarias, from his hiding-place, reaches out and takes the sword as Don Juan jumps into the room.*)

There! At last!

(*Dusting himself off and arranging his attire, without turning around*)

I could have split
My head with one fall!

(*Getting no response, he turns around casually.*)

I say... Where—

Diégarias (*revealing himself, approaching*)

Is it?
Your sword?... And I?...

(*Sarcastically*)

Inès?

Don Juan

Oh my!

Diégarias

Well, well,
Count!

(*Holding out the sword*)

Here we are!

Don Juan (*aside*)

Damn! Tricked!

Diégarias (*aside*)

My God, pray quell
My anger long enough, so that I not
Yield to my wrath and slay him on the spot!

(*To Don Juan, after a moment of silence*)

Let me be brief.

(*Trying unsuccessfully to control his emotions*)

I think you will agree
That it was less than wise, Excellency,
To dare set foot, at such an hour, within
These walls! Swordless, to boot!

Don Juan (*remaining very calm*)

To my chagrin,
My friend, I must confess there is much truth
In what you say. I should have known, forsooth,
That such as you would plan some infamy.

Diégarias (*enraged, bellowing*)

Oh!

Don Juan

And, as for my sword, it could not be
In better hands.

Diégarias

For smashing it, you mean!

(He breaks the blade over his knee and flings the pieces at Don Juan's feet.)

Don Juan (*pushing them aside with his toe, still very calmly*)
Well done...

Diégarias (*threatening*)
Quake, villain!

Don Juan
Ah, were I so green
As to be frightened by your threats, your roars,
And all that deadly earnest air of yours...

Diégarias (*shouting*)
Wretch!

Don Juan (*continuing, unconcerned*)
... then should I, perhaps, be moved, dear friend,
To beg for mercy. But—

Diégarias (*beside himself, growing more and more agitated*)
Enough! An end
To your insolence, your smug mockery!
No, count! Best mend your speech, and jeer at me
No more, else will you feel, without delay,
The power of my rightful wrath! No, stay
Your flippant tongue! I have you now! With one
Word, with one sign, so shall my will be done,
And I will wash in blood your scurrilous
Treachery!

(*Sarcastically*)

Ah! How fine and noble, thus,
These brave inheritors of greatness! These grandees,
Who, sullying their blazonry with lust
And lechery, hide beneath names august
Their infamous designs, and who—

Don Juan (*contemptuously, interrupting*)

Please, do
Come to the point!

(*There is a pause as Diégarias struggles to regain his composure.*)

Diégarias (*with deep emotion*)

The point?... I take it you
Still fail to comprehend! These tears that sear
My very soul... My pallor... My... My mere
Presence here, in this place... Does naught explain
The thought that tortures me and wracks my brain?

Don Juan

No, but I wait to learn.

Diégarias (*controlling his anger*)

You, count, have brought
Disgrace upon me, on my daughter... Wrought
Your vile—

Don Juan (*suddenly understanding, coldly, interrupting*)

Oh, that!...

Diégarias

Yes! And it falls to me—
A father, treated ignominiously—
Me, whose full sixty years, whose mien, whose station
Should have inspired, if not your admiration,
At least respect! Me, who toil for the weal
And fortune of the king, and all Castile!...
Yes, count, it falls to me to cleanse the shame
That you have heaped upon my house, my name!
For pity's sake, I pray you show remorse,
As loyalty demands, and that, perforce,
You now restore her honor to my child,
Her whom your ruse so grievously defiled,

By wedding her in proper wise. The priest
Awaits. All is prepared unto the least
Detail. Come to the chapel..

Don Juan

Sire...

Diégarias

Come... Come...

(*Taking his hand*)

I shall forget the past, my martyrdom,
Your wrongs, offenses... Rather shall you be
My second child, my son!

(*Raising his hand*)

See? Verily,
I swear it! Come...

Don Juan (*pulling his hand away*)

No, never! Never! This
Would seem to all an act of cowardice!
I cannot have it said—

Diégarias (*interrupting*)

You cannot?... You
Cannot, you say? Oh, if you only knew
What I... What I, for all my sixty years,
Can do to wash away my shame! Your fears
Would vanish, count!... Ah, but you jest.
Yes, surely would you be the scurviest
Of knaves, unholiest of villains, were
You to abuse a woman, toy with her,
Destroy her future, cast dishonor foul
Over her eighteen years, only to scowl

And turn aside, without deigning to look
Upon the tears of her whom you forsook
So shamelessly! No! From whatever race
You spring, you would not brook such a disgrace!
You cannot be so vile! Come...

Don Juan

Never! Never!...
Kill me! Do with me what you will, however
You would deprive me of my life! But be
Not so deceived by your self-flattery
As to believe that I, forgetting my
High birth, my pride, would ever choose to buy
My life with my dishonor! No! For when
Men yield to threats, for me they are not men
Worthy to bear their noble name!

Diégarias (*shouting, angrily*)

Ah! Curse
You! Curse you, then, you wretch! So much the worse
For you!

(*With profound sadness, musing to himself*)

My sixty summers have I spent,
Proud of my hair grown hoary white, content
Not to have any cause to hide within
My breast the slightest crime, the merest sin.
And now... Now must I take a life!

(*To Don Juan*)

The blame
Is on your head! You force me to it! Shame!
Shame, blackguard! Curse you!

(*Seizing his arm and pointing to a parchment on the table*)

Sign this document,
Or one and all will learn your fraudulent,
Scurrilous deed!

Don Juan (*pulling free*)
You must be mad.

Diégarias (*about to ring, but stopping, pointing*)
Behind
That door, the foulest of all humankind
Stands ready, waiting to appear, to kill
Without fear or remorse. And kill he will
Unless you do as I command! Reflect...

Don Juan (*sarcastically*)
I have done, thank you.

Diégarias (*handing him a quill*)
Sign... No disrespect
I mean, though bitterness and righteous ire
Master my civil tongue. However, sire,
I pray that you forget my words, and sign...

(*Urging the quill upon him*)

My quill...

Don Juan
Never!

Diégarias (*losing patience, shouting*)
What?

Don Juan
Never!

(*Sarcastically*)

I decline
Your offer.

Diégarias

My...? Good God almighty, he
Would seem intent to see his blood flow free!
What can I do? The very thought of it
Fills me with horror! Though I not commit
The deed myself, deserved it is, and I
Seal with his blood my secret.

(*Shouting toward the door*)

Enter!

(*Abul-Bekri enters quickly, a mask over his face and sword in hand. Don Juan recoils in spite of himself at the sudden appearance. Diégarias continues, threateningly.*)

Try
Not to escape! You cannot flee! All flight
Is useless...

Don Juan (*biting his lip*)

Flee? Hardly, old man. Despite
Your threats, I am quite calm... I wait until
It please your man to strike. Here I am. Kill
Me if you like, and without mercy. Thus
Shall all Castile see, as Diégarias
Sates, in my blood, his sullen enmity,
That he who holds the reins of state... Yes, he
Who for a dozen years has ruled, disbursed
The public treasure, shrinks not from the worst
Of crimes: assassination!

Diégarias

No, count! Be
Assured that, no less than your felony,
Your punishment will, in dark secrecy
Be hidden. None will ever hear a word
About one or the other!

Don Juan

Ah! You erred
In that regard. My felony, you say?
A secret?... Oh, no doubt you, come what may,
Have duly learned to keep a confidence.
But I, alas... No, all my friends know whence,
And why, and whither I set out, and what
I came to do! So, I say... Slay me, but
Be quick about it.

Diégarias (*to Abul-Bekri, pointing*)

Kill him!

Abul-Bekri

Ah!

(*As Abul-Bekri lunges at Don Juan to carry out the order, Diégarias stops him.*)

Diégarias

Wait!...

(*There is a long silence as Diégarias ruminates. Aside*)

Why?
What do I have to fear? Why must he die?
Wherefore need I six feet of earth to hide
The scandal of a crime known far and wide?
A crime that he admits!...

(*To Don Juan*)

You win!

Don Juan (*skeptically*)

Oh?

Diégarias

Yes.

(*Sarcastically*)

Fate, in all-wise, unwonted tenderness,
Decides another course for you, Don Juan.
Fear not my punishment. No, no! Live on!
Why need I, thus, the price of death exact,
Now that you have, yourself, revealed your act?
You are undone!

Don Juan

What will you do then?

Diégarias (*haughtily*)

Ah!

That will you learn, count, from the king.

(*At the door, upstage, calling*)

Holá!

Guard! Guard!

The Guard (*appearing at the threshold*)

Your Excellency?

Diégarias (*pointing to Don Juan*)

Take this man

Prisoner!

(*To Don Juan as he moves to resist*)

No, my friend! Nothing you can
Do now will be of any use to save
Your skin!

(*To The Guard*)

Take him, I said! Remove the knave
At once!

Don Juan (*hesitating for a moment, then to The Guard*)
Come...

(*Proudly*)

After you...

(*The Guard leaves and Don Juan follows him out.*)

SCENE 5

Diégarias, Abul-Bekri

Diégarias (*sitting down*)
Damnation! Shame!...
What good is it for me to bear the name
Of minister? What profits me my power
When, in my honor's most victorious hour,
I seem to feel his arrant words fall true
Upon my ears...

(*Apostrophizing*)

O you...

Abul-Bekri (*approaching him, aside*)
Now, between you
And me!

Diégarias (*continuing*)
You whom I serve in heart and mind,
For lo! these dozen years!... Who will not find
Another hand more loyal to support
The faltering state, more faithful to the court
And to Your Majesty... I place my trust
In you, O gracious king, and in your just,
Sagacious heart!

Abul-Bekri (*to Diégarias*)
A word, señor...

Diégarias (*noticing him*)
Abul-
Bekri!...

(*Getting up*)

Not now!

Abul-Bekri
One!

Diégarias
No, my heart is full.
I cannot listen.

Abul-Bekri (*authoritatively*)
But you must!

Diégarias (*taken aback*)
I...

(*Haughtily*)

Please
Remember who I am! Such liberties
Are not—

Abul-Bekri (*interrupting, coldly*)
Enough, señor! I wish to speak
With you!

Diégarias
I see! You wish...

(*Enraged*)

Scoundrel! You pique
My curiosity!

Abul-Bekri (*standing before him, continuing*)
And here, señor!
And now! For it is time. I wish no more
To suffer the indignities of my
Position silently. Too long have I
Served as your varlet, as your spy, and now
Even as your assassin... Though, I vow,
I have, for many a year, been privy to
A secret that, enriching me, could do
You grievous harm, señor.

Diégarias (*angrily*)
Oh? And what ought
That mean to me?

Abul-Bekri
Why, everything or naught!
You be the judge! It tells of one who hid

His name... A Jew, señor—heaven forbid!—
Who took a Christian name.

Diégarias (*trying to hide his concern, with a shudder*)
Ah?

Abul-Bekri
Yes. To hide
His cursèd race. But I thought best to bide
My time, and not speak of this tale until
Events demanded it. For good or ill...

Diégarias
Explain yourself. You speak in riddles.

Abul-Bekri
Oh?
Do I, señor? I thought that you might know
My tale. No matter. Let me be more clear...
Perhaps you will recall. It was the year
Fourteen hundred and thirty, and I was
Obliged to live in Greece, señor, because
My mistress—first of many!—dragged me there
Against my will. The life I had to bear
Was far from pleasant. Many a trade I had
To practice—merchant, soldier, smuggler—glad
To earn a crust. At length I came to be
A privateer. One feat of piracy
Yielded a store of booty that was well
Beyond my fondest hopes. And so, to sell
My share, I went to see a certain Jew,
Jacob Eliacin by name, but who
Deigned not receive me, treated me as though
I were, señor, the lowliest of the low,
And cast me off with great indignity.
From that day forth, before my eyes I see
His grotesque features, graven in my mind,

Eager to look on them again, to find
My Jew... And then... In Madrijal, where I
Had gone, a fortnight since, there to decry
A plot I had uncovered—how? God knows!—
Hatched by the admiral and one of those
Envoys of Rome... In Madrijal, I went
At once to see the minister, intent
On telling him, señor, all that I knew...
And lo! To my surprise, he was my Jew!

(*Sarcastically*)

You, Don Diégarias!

Diégarias

Me? Who...?

Abul-Bekri

Come, come!
Admit the truth! I pray you play not dumb,
My friend! Yes, you!... Ah, what a foe is fate!
Look upon me, in such a sorry state,
Whilst you, beneath a Christian name and guise,
Staunchest among His Majesty's allies,
His most respected, trusted counselor,
Have saved Seville from ravages of war
And civil strife... You, reaping, truth to tell,
Wealth from the lusts of a young ne'er-do-well
Who plies you with a fortune well beyond
Your need! And I, a lowly vagabond,
Living a life of squalid misery,
Who, for a ducat, would have willingly
Breathed my last breath, dragging my days along,
Unenvied...

Diégarias (*aside*)

What is it he wants?

Abul-Bekri (*continuing*)

But wrong
Am I to curse my fate and rail at God
For my condition. You, with but one nod—
Omnipotent!—can calm the storm, abate
The tempest, quell the violent winds of state.
Fortune have you. Immense... A retinue,
Lands, vassals, palaces... All for a Jew!
So be it. But I, with a single word,
Quick as a lightning flash, fast as a bird,
Could open wide, beneath you, an abyss
That would swallow it all, señor... All this,
And you as well, plunging you back into
The nothingness from which you sprang!

Diégarias (*boldly*)

Oh? Who
Stops you? Why will you do it not?

Abul-Bekri

Fie! Fie
On that! What good is it to me if I
Cause you to fall? No, no! A powerful
Diégarias means that his friend Abul-
Bekri is powerful no less! Should he
Tumble, I fall as well.

(*Sarcastically*)

Does he agree,
Señor?

Diégarias (*bitterly*)

I see... So, what you covet is
The wealth, position, and all that is his.

The servant's life tires you. You look askance
Upon it, and would fain command.

Abul-Bekri

Perchance...

Diégarias

And you desire, if I may be so bold,
To sell your silence for a pile of gold?

Abul-Bekri

Quite so! A pile... But that is not, señor,
All I require.

Diégarias

What?

Abul-Bekri

Ah, no... There is more.
Gold, in my hands, is much too quick, I fear,
To flow like water... Vanish, disappear,
Gone with the tide... One moment, rich... And then,
Farewell! Next moment, nothing, once again,
Alas!

Diégarias (*losing patience*)

What is it that you wish? Speak!

Abul-Bekri

Oh...
A place at court would suit me well.

Diégarias (*sarcastically*)

Ah, so...
A place at court! No more? You are quite sure

That it would be enough but to procure
A place at court?

Abul-Bekri

Why not? Tell me, is there
Something surprising in that thought?

Diégarias

You dare
Jest about such a matter? Surely you
Cannot speak seriously!

Abul-Bekri

I can, and do,
My friend! That is the price that you must pay
To buy my silence.

Diégarias (*after a heavy silence, scornfully*)

Vulgar popinjay!
You would have me inflict on king and court
An ignominy of the lowest sort,
Vile churl!

Abul-Bekri

Make up your mind, señor!

Diégarias (*aside*)

Damned be
The moment when I risked my destiny
Returning to Castile! Then, minister
And minion of the king—

Abul-Bekri (*interrupting his musings*)

What? You demur?

Diégarias

No, not demur... I...

(*Categorically*)

I refuse.

Abul-Bekri

Refuse?

Diégarias

Utterly!

Abul-Bekri

Think, my friend...

Diégarias

I cannot choose
To be unworthy of myself.

Abul-Bekri

But you—

Diégarias (*with disdain, pointing to the door*)

Leave!

Abul-Bekri (*standing defiantly before Diégarias, arms crossed*)

Yes, señor! But first...

(*With subdued rage*)

I have a few
Most pressing thoughts that I insist, before
I do, on sharing with our counselor
To king and court!... I know how much you loathe
The sight of me, how readily you clothe
Your scorn in insult and offensive tone.
I need but peer into your eyes alone
To see that sheer disdain that sends a chill
Throughout my body, boils my blood! What ill

Am I thus guilty of? Am I a Jew?
What? In my youth did I have naught to do
But flee to Greece? Have I been forced to stand,
Meekly, beneath some lackey's eager hand,
Raining its blows upon me for the court
To see?

Diégarias

But—

Abul-Bekri

Interrupt me not!... In short,
I walk with head held high, with pride. For sure
Am I that, if a pagan or a Moor—
Whatever I may be—I do not use
A Christian's name, my friend, to hide a Jew's,
And shame my ancestors!

Diégarias (*barely able to contain himself*)

You... Ah!

Abul-Bekri (*continuing*)

But yet
More must I tell you. For, lest you forget,
I, my friend, have no daughter, sinfully
Wronged by a fell, lascivious grandee,
And whom I have not yet avenged...

(*Moving to leave*)

And so,
Farewell for now!

Diégarias (*barring his exit*)

Too late! You cannot go
So easily,

(*With ironic emphasis*)

my friend! You have offended
A father's deepest grief. Let it be ended
Here and now! See?

(*Drawing his blade*)

Still can I wield the sword!
En garde!

Abul-Bekri (*disdainfully*)
I think not! You can ill afford
The risk.

(*With a touch of levity*)

And should you do me injury,
By chance...

(*Emphasizing*)

My friend, so much the worse for me!

Diégarias (*threatening*)
Oh? You would jest?

Abul-Bekri
Come, let me pass. I must
Be gone.

Diégarias (*holding his ground*)
Never!

Abul-Bekri
Very well, then! I trust
That window will suffice.

(*Going to the window*)

Till later...

Diégarias (*rushing over, trying unsuccessfully to prevent his escape*)
Ah!...
Hell and damnation!

(*As Abul-Bekri jumps out*)

Oh!...

(*Shouting out the window*)

Pérez! Holá!

Pérez's Voice
Sire?

Diégarias
Do your duty!

Abul-Bekri's Voice
Ayyy!... A trap!... Come, swine!
Defend yourself!

(*For several moments one can hear the exchange of blades, followed by a sharp cry from Abul-Bekri.*)

Aaaah!

(*There is a long silence.*)

Diégarias (*listening*)
Nothing?... God of mine!
Dear God of vengeance, be with me, I pray!

(There is another silence, then the sound of several voices outside the door. In spite of himself, Diégarias turns toward the source.)

Who comes?

(The door swings open and the king's page, Don Gaétan, appears, followed by a soldier.)

SCENE 6

Diégarias, Don Gaétan, then Pérez

Don Gaétan (*to Diégarias*)

Sire, I bear news. The alcalde
Of Avila arrives, and brings us very
Important word as the king's emissary.
His Majesty requires his counselor
Posthaste.

Diégarias (*aside*)

What? Leave?... How can I? Not before
I know if he is...

(*Pérez enters and approaches Diégarias.*)

Pérez (*to Diégarias, whispering*)

What I had to do
Is done, sire. He is dead.

Diégarias (*after pausing to collect himself, aside, sighing*)

Ah...

(*To Don Gaétan, pointing to the door*)

After you...

CURTAIN

Act 3

A hall in the Alcazar. Upstage, a corridor.

SCENE I

Don Gaétan, Don Sanche, The Commander, The Grandees

(*Don Gaétan is relaxing casually in an armchair. The others are standing about in the corridor.*)

Don Gaétan (*aside*)

His Majesty's advisers keep him penned
All morning!... Good! Then need we not attend
The mass today! So much the better!

Don Sanche (*apparently ill at ease to find him, approaching*)

Ah!

Marquis!

(*Motioning to the others to wait for him*)

The messengers from Avila
Bring us bad tidings.

Don Gaétan (*apparently unconcerned*)

Oh? They do?

Don Sanche

What? Know
You nothing of their dire report?

Don Gaétan (*standing up*)

What ho,

My friend! What need I know, except that my
Mistress is pink of flesh and blue of eye,
With long black tresses, and a coy, pert air,
And feet so small that I can hold them...

(*Holding out a hand*)

there!...

Both in one hand!

(*Taking Don Sanche by the arm, moving off with him*)

Carefree I live my days,
Eat when I choose, drink when I please, and praise
The twenty years of youth sparkling my glance!
Life is a pastime; love, a game of chance.
Need I know more?

(*Don Sanche leads him upstage, where he exits. Don Sanche and the others come downstage.*)

SCENE 2

Don Sanche, The Commander, The Grandees

Don Sanche

No doubt the minister
Will, for another hour or more, confer
On weighty issues with His Majesty.
Affairs of state... Besides, my page will be
Standing on guard outside their chambers. Thus
Can we, with utmost liberty, discuss
Our little matter... If I called you here,
In this unseemly place, it was not fear
Of your defection that so moved me, nor
The wish to tell you all what heretofore
Has come to pass. I know the strength of will
That beats within your breasts, and would no ill
Impute to you or to your courage. Nay,

Whatever dangers, perils, come our way,
Firm shall you be! No shadow shall becloud
Your brows, or make you shirk the glorious, proud
Mission before us! Furthermore, we are
Too far along our noble path... Too far
To dare turn back!

The Commander

Here, here!

Don Sanche (*continuing*)

Now, as you know,
Condemned to death, Don Luc and Don Pedro,
Hopeless, await their fate in chains. The reason?
Plotting against the crown. Despite their treason,
Confession could have saved their heads, invited
Clemency, but would surely have indicted
Us, their confederates. Thus did they choose,
Instead, to die. Let us not, then, misuse
Our brethren! Let us now reward their death
With blood, not tears. Unto our dying breath,
We have the means, my friends. We have the power.
Now is the time to act! Now is the hour!
The moment is at hand to challenge fate.
But rest assured, it is not senseless hate,
Blind rage, that moves me. No. Rather, I see
That now we have an opportunity
Unequaled. For, the news received last night
From Avila proves that the time is right:
Burgos is ready to erupt, amid
Reports of violence... Valladolid
As well... And Avila, whose suffering folk,
Chafing beneath taxation's heavy yoke,
Have, in their woe, chased out their governor,
Newly appointed, from their walls! What more
Need we to move our arms to act!

A Grandee

We need
Assurance that the risk will not exceed
Our means.

Don Sanche

Juan, king of Aragon—the second
Monarch to bear that royal name—has reckoned
Five thousand soldiers for our cause. Navarre
Promises us three thousand... Brave they are,
And know no fear, intrepid... And, however
Frightful and fierce the combat, they shall never
Retreat!

The Commander

What forces have we now at hand?

Don Sanche

The prince's partisans, my own, yours...

The Commander

And?

Don Sanche

A province that stands ready to provide
The cause with ten score lancers, true and tried.

The Commander

No more?

Don Sanche

And fortresses... Some half a dozen,
Held by our friends. And if, perchance, our cousin
Aragon should defect and quit us, we
Can still count on Toledo, certainly,
And Salamanca too, without a doubt.

Avila likewise, which will carry out
Toledo's wishes, lying to the west
Of it, and sharing in its interest.

The Commander

So, think you it behooves us to proceed
At once?

Don Sanche

If it be done, best do the deed
Without delay. The longer we may wait,
The more we give a chance to vacillate
To traitors in our midst. What profits it
To hesitate? Rather the opposite
Should be our aim. In these perfidious times,
Inaction and the host of heinous crimes
It breeds weigh on our heads, and ought to make
Us quake. When we have but one step to take
To reach our goal, let us eschew the pleasure
Of halting, dawdling on the way, at leisure!
Struggle we must against our enemy.
And who is that, you ask? Nay, not Henri,
That weakling, whom one breath, one gust of wind
Would fell! No... That astute, well-disciplined,
Sharp-eyed, quick-witted minister of his!
That who-knows-what?, whose only object is
To compromise our power, to bring us down,
And make us all subservient to the crown.
So wished he yesterday, and wishes still
Today no less. Such men persist until
Time works their will. He must be stopped!

The Commander

And soon!

We all agree. The time is opportune...

(*To The Grandees*)

To work!...

Don Sanche (*catching sight of his page*)
Ah! Shhh!... My page... Quiet! The king
Comes from the council-chamber.

(*Softly*)

Everything
Is ready...

(*With a glance heavenward*)

Bless us!...

(*Continuing*)

The Del Oro Tower,
Tonight!... I shall wait there... You know the hour...

(*They all line up along the corridor. The King enters, followed by Diégarias.*)

The King (*to Don Sanche*)
The messengers have left?

Don Sanche

Yes, Majesty...

(*On a gesture from The King, Don Sanche, The Commander, and The Grandees leave.*)

SCENE 3
The King, Diégarias

The King
No sadness, please... If anyone should be

Ashamed, count, certainly it is not you.
Nor is it your pure child Inès. You two
Are blameless in the matter. His alone
The infamy! He who, shameless, has shown
Himself to be without a soul, without
The slightest worth, yet whom you are about
To honor with your fortune and redeem
With your good name.

Diégarias

Your Majesty's esteem
Pleases me.

The King

We shall see...

Diégarias

He comes. I pray
You act with prudence.

The King

Fear not. I need say
A single word to make him pay for such
An ignominious deed! Your torments touch
Me quite as much as you.

Diégarias

He may refuse.

The King

Refuse? Perchance. But his it is to choose
His fate...

(*Looking upstage*)

Look, count. He comes... Go now.

I am the king, and I shall not allow
A friend to suffer unavenged.

(*Diégarias nods, and leaves, as Don Juan enters, upstage.*)

SCENE 4
The King, Don Juan

The King (*to Don Juan, sharply*)

Come here,
You!

Don Juan (*aside*)

Ah! That tone...

(*Aloud, without moving*)

Sire?

The King (*pointing*)

Here! And now!

Don Juan (*aside*)

I fear
He knows...

(*Approaching, to The King*)

Your Majesty?

The King

Listen to me!
Don Pedro and Don Luc, by my decree,
Have been arrested. And, my dear Don Juan,
Within the hour, or less, our Don Guzmán
De Castro shall be languishing as well

In prison. As for you, another cell
Is being readied as we speak.

(*Sarcastically*)

For, your
Collusion as an arch conspirator
Against my house, against my crown, will not
Go unrewarded!

Don Juan

Sire—

The King (*interrupting*)

No, no! Your plot
Has been unmasked, count. And you know, no doubt,
The punishment that must be meted out
To traitors, and the horror that befalls
Their kind. Within the dungeon's solid walls,
You shall await—with but a priest to say
A blessing on your head—that fatal day.
Then, barefoot, up the steps... A final prayer...
The scaffold, standing in the city square...

Don Juan (*aside*)
Confound him!

The King (*continuing*)

And the noose!

Don Juan (*aloud*)

Sire...

The King

There is more,
Don Juan!... Please bear in mind, this is your third
Offense against the crown. With but one word,

Despite your rank, if I so chose, I might...
Before the hangman has his chance to blight
Your name forever...

(*Sarcastically*)

I might grace your line's
Blasonry with a gibbet! My designs,
I hope, are clear!... Unless, that is...

(*Don Juan gives a quizzical look.*)

Unless,
Before me, here and now, you acquiesce
To mend one of your crimes, redeem a life,
And make the wronged Doña Inès your wife.

Don Juan

Your Majesty... Sire...

The King

Silence! Think on it!
You have a quarter hour.

(*He leaves.*)

SCENE 5

Don Juan (*alone*)

Ah! Were more fit
The death proposed for such as me... The blade,
The pyre... I should not waver. Unafraid,
I should die willingly. But oh! The shame
Of climbing to the scaffold!... All the same,
To marry her, whose very name bespeaks
Some upstart vile!... "Diégarias" ... It reeks
Of commonness!... And I, count and grandee

Of Spain... To wallow in such infamy!
Ah no! My blood, my honor will not let
Me sink so low that I forsake, forget
My name!... And yet... His threat is real, I know.
Never before has he addressed me so
Angrily!... What? Have I a choice? If I
Would live I must accept his terms, comply
This very day! God! What a tale is this!
Can no one save me from this dark abyss
That swallows me? Am I unmanned, undone?
Alas! If there were someone, anyone...
I would give him my fortune, to the last
Doubloon!

(*During the last few moments a cloaked and hooded figure has entered, surrounded by Don Sanche, The Commander, and the other Grandees, among them The Inquisitor. At Don Juan's final words he throws off his hood, revealing Abul-Bekri.*)

Abul-Bekri (*to Don Juan*)
No need for that!

SCENE 6

Abul-Bekri, Don Juan, Don Sanche, The Commander, The Inquisitor, The Grandees

Don Juan (*turning round*)
Who...? What...?

Abul-Bekri (*to Don Juan*)
Hold fast
Your fortune, count! I come to save you, not
To take your wealth.

Don Juan (*to Abul-Bekri, taking his hand*)
Bless you, my friend! But what—

Abul-Bekri (*interrupting*)

Your tongue is rather quick to give its blessing,
Señor! This hand... This hand that you are pressing,
Yesterday could have killed you!

(*Don Juan lets go his hand.*)

Ah! I see
You understand!

Don Juan

You! But...

Abul-Bekri

No, certainly,
At this, my proudest hour, by God above—
By Allah, count—surely it is not love
That makes me save a Christian!

(*Leaning against an armchair*)

I have fought
With destiny... Derision... Sore distraught,
And near gone mad at times!... For thirty years,
Yearning, with many a thought that tortures, sears
The soul... For thirty years, I plot, I plan
The downfall, the undoing of one man.
And when the moment comes to strike... Too late!
I might have stabbed the swine! Yet unkind fate
Did not agree... But now, my infidel
Shall feel my wrath! Whatever torments hell
Reserves for me, my hate will have its day,
At long last!

Don Juan

But, good stranger, if I may...
What brings you to this place?

Abul-Bekri

I come, Don Juan,
To ease my soul and wreak my vengeance!

Don Juan

On...?

Abul-Bekri

Diégarias!

Don Juan (*surprised*)

Diégarias? What ill
Has he done you?

Abul-Bekri

What ill?

(*Opening wide his cloak, exposing his bloody chest*)

Come, look your fill,
My friend!

(*As Don Juan makes a move toward him, he sits down, obviously weak, continuing to speak with difficulty.*)

What ill indeed!... So! Now you see
The answer to your question!... Destiny
Decreed—so it was written—that last night
His servant almost slew me!... And he might
Have done... Yes, heaven knows he surely tried...
But for Allah, I doubtless would have died,
There, on the spot. For, thinking I was dead,
He left me where I lay... Ah, but instead,
At length...

(*Clutching his breast*)

Ayyy!... Oh! The pain...

Don Juan

Good God!

Abul-Bekri (continuing)

At length,
Pressing my wound, summoning up what strength
I had, I crawled, snake-like, without a sound,
Seething with rage... There, by the shore, I found
Your barque... I crawled inside, lay suffering, still,
And let the current bear me, do its will...
I wished to see the king, recently come
Home from Triana... Then, in time, through some
Fair stroke of chance, the alcalde came by,
Spied me... And here I am...

(*He collapses.*)

Don Juan

My friend!...

Abul-Bekri (with great effort, straightening up)

But die
I shall not!... No, I vow! Not yet!... It is
Not Allah's will that this servant of his
Perish before you learn what brings me here.

Don Juan

Explain...

Abul-Bekri (clutching his breast)

Ah!...

Don Juan

You were saying...

Abul-Bekri

Yes... Give ear,

And you shall know...

(*As he is about to reveal his secret, The Page enters.*)

The Page (*announcing*)

His Majesty!

Abul-Bekri (*as The Grandees hurriedly gather round to conceal him*)

Damnation!

(*The King enters, followed by Don Gaétan, who remains upstage, and The Archbishop.*)

SCENE 7

The King, Don Gaétan, Abul-Bekri, Don Juan, Don Sanche, The Commander, The Archbishop, The Inquisitor, The Grandees

The King (*to Don Juan, approaching him*)

Your answer!... I await your declaration,
Don Juan! What will it be?

Don Juan (*aside*)

What can I say?

(*Aloud, to The King, hesitating*)

Your Majesty...

The King (*sharply*)

Come, come! Enough delay!
Reply!

Don Juan (*resigned*)

I... I agree.

The King

So be it, then!

(*As he affixes his seal to a parchment, to Don Juan*)

Count, your betrothed...

(*Abul-Bekri, still concealed by The Grandees, manages to whisper something hurriedly in Don Juan's ear.*)

Don Juan (*to Abul-Bekri, in a whisper*)
What?...

(*As Inès enters, followed by Diégarias, The Archbishop, and Ladies-in-Waiting*)

Tell me that again!

The King (*taking Inès's hand, respectfully*)
Come, come, my virtuous child. Hold high your head,
You, pure of heart, of soul, worthy to wed
A prince!

SCENE 8

The King, Don Gaétan, Abul-Bekri, Don Juan, Don Sanche, The Commander, The Archbishop, The Inquisitor, Inès, Diégarias, The Grandees, Ladies-in-Waiting

Diégarias (*to The King, in a whisper*)
Thank you, Your Majesty!

(*To Inès*)

Please, try
To hide your sadness...

Abul-Bekri (*aside, weakly*)

Ah... So... Now is my
Vengeance complete!

Don Gaétan (*to The King, pointing to the marriage contract, on the table*)

All is in readiness.

The King

Good! Then we may proceed.

(*To Inès, presenting the parchment*)

Doña Inès...
Your wedding present!

Inès

Sire...

The King

Naught want I more
Than to assure your happiness. Therefore,
To you I give this document, whereby,
Should Don Juan try my royal patience, I
Place in your hands his fate.

Inès (*taking the parchment, to The King*)

Sire, if you please...

(*Examining it while The King goes to the table to sign the marriage contract. Aside, surprised*)

No writing... Not a word! His Majesty's
Carte blanche!

(*She places the parchment in her bosom.*)

The King (*after signing, presenting his quill to The Archbishop*)
Your Grace!

(*The Archbishop signs, returns the quill, which The King presents to Don Juan.*)

Now you, Don Juan!

Don Juan (*approaching*)

I do
Not wish to disobey or anger you
Before the court, Your Majesty. But truly,
I cannot sign.

The King (*sharply*)
What?

Diégarias (*aside*)
Ah! Some outrage newly
Plotted to break my will!

The King (*to Don Juan*)
Count! What means your
Refusal? You cannot...?

Don Juan
No. I assure
Your Majesty. I neither can nor ought.

The King
And why?

Don Juan
Never be said that I have brought
Shame and disgrace upon my house, and lost
My Christian soul, however great the cost!
Even, Your Majesty, my very life!

The King (*commanding*)
Explain!

Don Juan
I cannot, will not take to wife...
I, Count Don Juan, of old and noble race...
No, sire, I will not take to wife some base
Vile Jewess!

Inès (*aside*)
God!

Diégarias (*aside*)
Ah, no!

The King (*to Don Juan, not believing his ears*)
Some what? You said...
Some what?

Don Juan
A Jewess!... No, I will not wed...
The daughter of...

(*Pointing to Diégarias*)

Jacob Eliacin!

The King
Who?

Diégarias (*aside*)
Woe! Ah, woe!

The King (*to Don Juan, pointing to Diégarias*)
Him?

(*To Diégarias*)

What say you? What mean

His words?

(*Diégarias remains silent.*)

What? Say you nothing?

Don Juan (*to The King*)

Sire, why ask?

What can he say, save that I now unmask
His treachery! Save that, Your Majesty,
Years ago, in our palace, publicly,
Two of our lackeys throttled him!

The King (*pointing to Diégarias*)

Him?

Diégarias (*reaching for his dagger*)

Oh!

(*To Don Juan, barely containing himself*)

Who told you this? Who, count? Who? I must know!
His blood... His blood shall answer for this shame!
His name, count! Speak! Tell me! Tell me his name!

Abul-Bekri (*pushing aside The Grandees, stepping forward*)
Abul-Bekri!

Diégarias (*recoiling*)

Good God! Him?... How—

Abul-Bekri (*to Diégarias*)

Ah yes!

Quake, shudder, traitor! It is I!... None less

Than I, Abul-Bekri!... Ghost, spectre, whom
Your villainy dispatched! Back from the tomb
To trample you beneath my feet!...

(*As Diégarias, shaken, stands with eyes downcast*)

You cower,
Old man? You tremble, shake, to see your power
Vanish before your eyes? Are you afraid
To look upon the breast where your foul blade
Dealt its fell blow?

(*To The King and The Grandees, pointing to Don Juan*)

It is the truth, as he,
Don Juan, has spoken it, Your Majesty!
The pure truth!

Diégarias (*enraged*)
Oh!

Abul-Bekri (*growing weaker as he speaks*)
I have but little breath
To waste. Nor would I dare defile my death
With lies. No, he...

(*Pointing to Don Juan*)

He speaks the truth, I swear!

(*Pointing to Diégarias*)

Let him do likewise!

(*To Diégarias, with insolent sarcasm*)

Yes, you! Do you dare?

You, who know only virtue! You, whose heart
Has made of its sincerity an art
For all these years!

Diégarias (to The King)

What? Can it be? Here, in
The Alcazar, before your throne, within
Sight of your crown, whose glory I alone
Raised to its heights of splendor, never known...
Here must I stand, Your Majesty, the while,
And listen to the insults that a vile,
Impudent lackey hurls and flings at me!
What, sire? Despite my virtue, earnestly,
Loudly proclaimed... Despite my fame... Despite
My deep, selfless devotion, day and night...
Despite all I have done these dozen years...
Services past, services present... Tears
Of pain, shed with my blood, more than a score
Of times, to keep the empire strong... And now,
When I am dealt a vicious blow, you bow
Your head? You look away...?

(*He pauses.*)

Nothing?... Have you
Nothing to say?

(*He pauses again before The King's obstinate silence.*)

So be it.

(*Resigning himself*)

But I do!...
One thing have I, Your Majesty...

(*Addressing The Grandees*)

One thing
To say before you all... And to my king,
Forsooth... The scoundrel speaks the truth. I am
A Jew.

(*Abul-Bekri cannot repress a gesture of joy. At the same time, Inès is visibly shaken.*)

The King (*angrily, to Diégarias*)
Deceiver!... What? You are a sham?
You...

Diégarias (*to The King*)
Please, Your Majesty! Condemn me not
So quickly! Have I not the right—

The Inquisitor (*interrupting, sarcastically*)
The what?
A Jew?

Diégarias (*continuing*)
... to speak in my defense?

The Inquisitor (*to The King*)
Sire, mind
Not what he says! In you the Christ must find
Strength and support! You are a Christian!

Diégarias (*continuing*)
Sire,
Let me but say—

The Inquisitor (*to Diégarias, gesticulating*)
Back, devil! Back!... Hell's fire
Burns in your breath, and would our souls consume!

(*Raising his arms to heaven*)

Great God! You who see all, who all illume,
Who hold the fate of mortals in your hands,
Who rule the destiny of all the lands
That flourish here below, and who strike fear
And terror with your law... How could you, here,
Amongst us, let this living blasphemy,
This miserable Jew, so shamelessly
And brazenly clothe his black wretchedness
Beneath a regal mantle?

(*To Diégarias*)

You! Confess
Your impious deed! For now, at last, must you
Pay for your sacrilege! Tremble, base Jew!
Gaze at the boldness of your crime!

Inès (*to The Inquisitor*)

Sire, please...
I pray you—

The Inquisitor (*ignoring her, continuing*)

Wickedest of treacheries,
Hiding behind a name not yours, no more
Shall you conceal the one that once you bore,
Or claim—falsest of falsities!—to be
A Christian!

Inès (*to The Inquisitor*)

Sire...

The Inquisitor (*to Diégarias, continuing*)

Be cursed!

Inès (*throwing herself at his feet in supplication*)

No! Hear my plea!
I... I beseech you! Curse him not, but show

The mercy that our Savior would bestow...
The very God of whom you speak! Pray set
Aside your righteous ire! Ah, mercy! Let
Your heart be moved with pity for our plight!
My fate and his are one... Sire, you are right.
My father... Yes, he is a Jew. But why
Must I, a Christian, feel your wrath?

(*She pauses, waiting for a reply.*)

Sire?

The Inquisitor (*archly*)

I
Have spoken!

Diégarias (*to Inès, taking her hand*)

Child, be brave. I am a Jew,
And cursed. Such is God's will. What may ensue
Only He knows. But I must bear alone
The woes that destiny, alas, has sown
Upon my path. Ah, but my soul is strong.
It shall withstand this new affront. But wrong
Were it for you to bear it with me. Thus
I bid you leave, and with your generous
And loving soul, follow your Christian heart.
Go... Let me be, Inès. For we must part.

Inès

Go, father? Leave you? Part?... Why speak you so?
God, in His mercy, has no anger, no
Contumely for the child who, loyally,
Fulfills, unto the end, her duty.

(*Emphasizing*)

We
Must part... Together, father... Let me share
With you the burden of your deep despair.

Diégarias (*taking her in his arms*)
Inès! My child!

Inès
Come, let us leave this place
Of woe.

(*As they are about to leave, Diégarias stops. Unable to control his emotion, he flings himself before The King, who is deep in reflection.*)

Diégarias
Mercy, sire!

(*Embracing The King's knees*)

Mercy for my race,
My honor!

(*Pointing to Inès*)

Mercy, above all, for her,
My child! She is a Christian!

(*The King remains silent, contemplating.*)

You demur...
I beg you, sire, abandon not your servant,
Him who, these many years, has, with a fervent,
Solemn devotion, plied your cause! My tears
Could wash away all traces of those years
Of loyal, faithful service! Mercy, sire!
Save her, Your Majesty!

(*Carried away with emotion, grasping The King's hand*)

Let not your ire—

The King (*withdrawing his hand, sharply*)
Unhand me, Jew!

Diégarias
Sire, pity! Please!... One day
You shall be old as I am... You shall pay
Life's price to time. Pray, in your father's name,
And in your God's, and...

(*With a gesture toward the assembled gathering*)

in your court's... Disclaim

(*Pointing to The Inquisitor*)
His inhumanity!

The King (*coldly*)
I can do naught
For you!

Diégarias
Sire...

The King
Rise!

Diégarias (*in desperation*)
But sire...

The King (*impatiently*)
Rise!

Diégarias (*rising, but with a supplicating gesture*)
But—

The King (*sarcastically*)
I thought
I said—

Diégarias (*interrupting*)
I know... I...

(*Making a final attempt to move him*)

But, Your Majesty...

(*Pointing to Inès*)

For her!

The King
Her... You... It matters not to me!

Diégarias (*resigned, somberly*)
Then have I nothing more to say.

Abul-Bekri (*who has been watching with growing joy, despite his weakness*)
At last!
I die content!

(*He slumps over, dead. Diégarias is surrounded by several angry Grandees.*)

The Commander (*to Diégarias, reacting to his last statement*)
Best is it that your past
Remain unspoken, Jew! And you do well
To say no more. But we have much to tell...
We, Christians, who, aghast at a perverse

And noxious fate, accepted—nay, far worse,
Reveled in—honors that your shameless hand
Bestowed upon us! Ah, sham contraband,
These honors now! They sully and defile
Our names! False marks of grandeur from a vile,
Ignoble Jew!

(*The Grandees mutter their approval.*)

The First Grandee

Quite so!

The Second Grandee

Here, here!

The Third Grandee

Agreed!

The First Grandee

Verily does he speak the truth!

The Commander (*continuing*)

Indeed,

Myself, Juan de la Raza, I became
Duque de Torres, owing to my fame—
Proud man-at-arms, intrepid cavalier—
In wresting from the Moorish yoke Cahir,
Gibraltar, Archidona, Baena,
Marbella... And, with many a loud huzzah,
You it was, who, conferring my reward,
Placed in my eager grasp...

(*Holding up his sword*)

this very sword!

(*Brandishing it*)

Ah! Watch what now I do with it! Look!

(*Breaking the blade over his knee*)

See?

No present from a Jew shall tarnish me
Or cast dishonor on these hands!

(*Flinging the two halves down at Diégarias's feet, disdainfully*)

Fie! Fie

On it!

The First Grandee

And when, with valiant prowess, I
Defended Zahara with great éclat,
You placed the green cross of Alcantara
About my neck!

(*Ripping the cross from his neck as he speaks, and flinging it at Diégarias's feet*)

Bah! Now no more, I swear,
Will this, my Christian flesh, suffer to wear
Anything you have given me... You, old,
Unclean descendant of the race that sold
Mankind's redeemer!

(*Diégarias, who has remained silent and motionless, slowly crosses the stage and approaches Don Sanche, who is standing at the opposite extreme.*)

Diégarias (*to Don Sanche, with a mixture of scorn and sarcasm*)

Now, Don Sanche, I warrant
You too must have a properly abhorrent
Message to fling at me! You, whom I made
A knight with my own hands, choosing your blade,
Your cross myself... You, whom I brought to court,

Raised a grandee... No doubt you can distort
My deeds in some befitting fashion! You,
Who, young and fearless, with your derring-do,
Saved the king's very life in battle, and
On whom I lavished castles, fiefdoms, land,
Everything!... Surely you cannot stand by
In silence, and refuse to vilify
My kindnesses! So, speak! I wait to hear
Your noble words of gratitude!

Don Sanche (*to Diégarias, in a whisper*)
Draw near
And listen well.

(*As Diégarias complies*)

Three days from now, or less,
An old man will appear to you, López
By name, sent there by me. If you desire
Revenge upon your enemies, then, sire,
Go where he leads.

Diégarias (*in a whisper, replying*)
Where?

Don Sanche (*continuing to whisper throughout*)
To my house...

Diégarias (*likewise*)
But—

Don Sanche
There
Shall I assist you.

Diégarias

Pity my despair,

Don Sanche...

Don Sanche (*still in a whisper*)

Courage! In three days shall we meet.

(*He turns and leaves.*)

Diégarias (*to Inès, taking her hand*)

Vengeance was mine!

(*Looking to heaven*)

Now be it twice as sweet!

(*He and Inès go off.*)

CURTAIN

Act 4

Diégarias's chambers. Upstage, a corridor and a door. Stage left, a window and a chair. Stage right, a lamp. It is night. The room is in shadows.

SCENE I

Inès is onstage, deep in thought. Pérez enters.

Pérez (*aside, looking at Inès, shaking his head*)
Tsk tsk! Poor child!

(*To Inès, approaching her*)

When comes my master, pray
Give him this letter, and without delay,
For it was brought in greatest haste.

Inès

By whom?

Pérez
A beggar...

(*Giving her the letter*)

Here...

Inès
Pérez, can we assume
That what we hear is true? About the king,
I mean.

Pérez

Most true!

Inès

Oh? Tell me everything!

Pérez

Yesterday, with great boldness, the grandees
Chased him from power, and, making quick to seize
The throne, proclaimed for all to hear that he
Was now bereft of all authority,
And that he was no more the king! And so,
With the archbishop and the nuncio,
The court decreed that Don Alphonse was now
King of Castile. And that, indeed, is how
It came about, as best I know...

Inès

Aha...

Pérez

Outside the very walls of Avila.

Inès

What says the populace of what transpired?

Pérez

Nothing, it seems...

(*He notices Diégarias about to enter.*)

Your father...

(*Diégarias enters, pale and dejected. He throws his cape and cloak onto the chair. Pérez bows to him and leaves.*)

SCENE 2

Diégarias, Inès, then Pérez

Inès (*aside*)

Oh, how tired
He looks! How sad his mien!

(*Aloud, to Diégarias*)

Where, father dear...
Where have you been? Long have you left me here
Alone, waiting and wondering.

Diégarias (*with deep sadness*)

I know
Not where I wandered... Up, down, to and fro...
So deep my woe, so bitter my chagrin,
My head knows scarcely where my feet have been...
Here, there... Aimless I walked! The cool night air
Calming my fevered brow... My dark despair...

(*He pauses, noticing the letter she has in her hand.*)

What are you holding? What is that, Inès?
A letter?

Inès

It was given to Pérez
Moments ago.

Diégarias (*taking it, reading*)

"In one hour, to your door
Shall come a friend, whose fate forevermore—
His life or death—is in your hands."

(*Throwing the latter down on the table*)

A friend!

(*Sitting down, musing*)

Three days... And now that time is at an end.
With every hour my head has bled its pain,
Waiting for one... Waiting, alas, in vain.
O grief! How deep the change that you have wrought
In my existence! Ah! Who would have thought...
And all about, revolt and insurrection,
Destroying what once stood!... In my dejection,
Vainly I plumb my past, in all its length
And breadth, to find some source of virtue, strength,
Some God-inspired perfection that might be
A balm to soothe my wound, to comfort me
And quench the burning grief... To scar my heart
Quickly, against the ache, the searing smart
It feels. Yet naught I find in me but hate!

(*He pauses.*)

O destiny! I cannot extricate
Myself, cast off the chains you wrap about
Me, in my darkness! Fate, why do you flout
And taunt me? Can it be that, in this time
Of mournful sorrow, terror, fearsome crime;
When civil war rends us apart; when all
Our cities rise up, ready soon to fall
Under the weighty sway of Aragon,
Whose minions in Castile will spread anon
Their message; when Granada, vowing our
Destruction, threatens daily to devour
The capital; when everyone, tired, bent
Beneath life's burdens, loathes the government
And welcomes a revolt... What? Can it be
That I alone, a Jew, powerlessly

Imprisoned in my rage, wearing a vile
Mark on my brow, and bearing my exile,
Banished with hue and cry, shall nonetheless
Live on in shame and useless nothingness!...

Inès

Father...

Diégarias (*to Inès*)

Today, we spoke of country, you
And I, and of the noble heroes, through
The ages, whom the past bequeaths to us.
But why? What folly is it to discuss
Such things! Is there a fatherland for those
Who have no rights? Tomorrow, if I chose
To put aside my pride and, humbly, go
Trembling before His Majesty... Bow low
And deep before our Christian king... Yes, him
Whom I sustained, defended, life and limb,
For many a year... If I begged, on my knees,
Hands clasped in prayer: "O gentle monarch, please,
Help me! Many are they who now would seize
My wealth, my property... Who would divest
Me of my very life! Pray, save me, lest
I die anon!..." What think you would result?
Ah! How his rogues would mock me and exult
To chase away this Jew, so mad with pride,
That he knows not he ought be satisfied
Merely to live, and who, base citizen
Deprived of rights and lowliest of men,
Dares to invoke the justice of our laws!
So would it be!

Inès

Ah, father! You it was
Who raised them up! And this is how they show
Their gratitude!

Diégarias (*nodding*)

I know, Inès... I know...

(*Pérez enters and remains upstage.*)

Inès

Forget them, father!

(*There is a brief silence. Diégarias takes his head in his hands as if to dispel his thoughts, then motions to Pérez to approach.*)

Pérez (*to Diégarias*)

Master?

Diégarias (*to Pérez*)

In a few
Moments a man will come. Be sure that you
Show him in promptly.

Pérez

Who?

Diégarias

I cannot say,
Pérez. I know not...

(*He motions Pérez off.*)

Pérez

Ah...

(*He leaves.*)

Inès (*to Diégarias*)

I hope you may
Trust in this stranger.

Diégarias (*indifferently*)

So his message says.
He claims to be a friend.

Inès

What services
Seeks he from you?

Diégarias

My help...

Inès

You say he claims
To be a friend. But, father, friends have names,
And he has written none. Besides, can one
Be sure the hand is his? Or has he done
Something to alter it?

Diégarias

What difference—

Inès

An elder, long of years, has no defense
Against a rogue who dares do what he will.

Diégarias

Would one who seeks my help do me much ill,
My child?

Inès

No... But... How do you know that he
Is not a foe, bent on some treachery?...
Some wretched enemy, who puts to use
His clever guile to find you?... Who, by ruse
And wile, enters your very home?

Diégarias

Why should
Anyone wish to end my days? What good
Would come of it? Have I a noble name?
Have I a rank that someone could proclaim
Now to be his? Am I one of those rare,
Privileged beings who, on their foreheads wear
Three hundred years of glorious legacy
Without a single day of infamy
To cloud their brow?

(*Sinking back into his reverie*)

Ah, fate! What games you play!
Yesterday, clad in purple... And today,
Cast down into the mire!...

Inès

Pray, father, be
Not quick to trust this stranger!

Diégarias (*continuing his musing, not listening to her*)

Banished! Me,
Diégarias!... Who saved the faltering state
When the ambitions of a growing spate
Of warring factions spread their chaos round
About!... When, with each passing hour, one found
Some new attack upon the future, some
Treasonous deed that bade fair to become
The final blow, the last ignoble act!...
And all the while the treasury was sacked,
Pillaged by vicious hands! They would have sold
The king himself for a few coins of gold!

Inès (*trying to calm him*)

Father dear...

Diégarias (*ignoring her*)

Ah, but then... I know not by
What miracle!... God looked down from on high
And kindled in my soul the inspiration,
Somehow, to bring to life this dying nation,
And so transformed the Jew—unknown, obscure—
Into the minister whose skills assure
The realm's salvation, cure its ills... Again,
The empire—like a runner, stopping when
The course grows harsh, but who, with flanks grown strong,
Takes up the race once more—plunges headlong
Into the future, flourishing reborn
Beneath my stalwart hand... And I, forlorn,
Am banished!

Inès

God above!

Diégarias (*continuing, growing more and more despondent*)

Ah, what a fool
Was I, to think my strength, my power could rule
The empire's future! Clear the task I set
Myself withal, and great the cost of sweat
And blood!... But I relented not! My goal?
To find the way to unify Spain's soul,
Join small with great—her principalities,
Counties, and duchies—and between two seas
Build here an empire in the name of Spain,
Worthy of one the likes of Charlemagne!...
And I am banished...

Inès

Ah, good God above!

(*To Diégarias*)

Would that my blood might, with the gift of love,

Bring you the solace that your dark despair
Demands!

Diégarias (*taking her hand*)
My child...

Inès
What? Can your tongue yet bear
To call me thus? Do I still have the right
To claim myself my father's child, despite
A daughter's failure to console his grief
And guide his trembling steps?... When, like a thief,
I stole the honor from his whitening head,
Fouled by the breath of my fell deed?... When, led
Astray...

Diégarias
Please, Inès... Please! My heart may bleed
And break with my distress, but never need
My sad recriminations bring a blush
Of shame to smirch your tender cheek! So hush,
My child! Repentance cleanses and redeems
You of your fault, however base it seems.
Come... Lift your eyes. Be not, I pray, so glum.
I pardon you!... I love you!

(*He embraces her. After a moment of silence, Pérez enters.*)

SCENE 4
Diégarias, Inès, Pérez

Pérez (*to Diégarias*)
Sire, there come
Two men to see you.

Diégarias (*to Pérez*)
Two?

Pérez

Yes. And they wear
Masks on their faces.

Diégarias

Masks? What need is there
For masks when one comes here? Why must one, thus,
Appear distrustful and mysterious
When one would seek my help?

Pérez

Some are there, sire,
Of such a high degree that they desire
Not to allow their woes to see the light
Of day.

Diégarias

What are you saying?

Pérez

Sire, I might
Have been deceived, but...

Diégarias (*sharply, in a whisper*)

Yes? What...?

Pérez (*hesitating*)

I... I thought...

Diégarias

Go on!

Pérez

Sire, I believed, when my eye caught
Sight of the stranger, that... I thought that he
Might be none other than His Majesty!

Diégarias

The king?

Pérez

I would have sworn it, sire!

Diégarias

The king!...
Whose brow already feels the tottering,
Teetering crown, about to fall, and who
Finds none but me, of all his retinue,
To save his throne!... O demons born of hell!
Condemn me, damn me to a fare-thee-well,
But let it be! My blood, my life are yours
If only... Ah!

(*To Pérez*)

Pérez! Fling wide the doors
And show them in! I shall see to the rest!

Pérez

Yes, sire. At once...

(*He leaves.*)

Diégarias (*to Inès*)

My child, I think it best
You leave us.

Inès

But...

Diégarias

You need not fear!

Inès

I go,

But...

Diégarias

Please...

(*Inès leaves reluctantly. The two Masked Men enter. The second remains upstage, in the background, while the first approaches Diégarias.*)

SCENE 5

Diégarias, the two Masked Men

The Masked Man (*nodding, to Diégarias*)

May God protect you!

Diégarias (*recognizing his voice, aside*)

Ah! I know

That voice!... Yes, it is he!

The Masked Man (*aside*)

O mask! Lie tight
About my face, and hide my shame this night!
And you, O noble ancestors, conceal
The infamy I bring upon Castile
And all the royal line!

Diégarias (*offering him a chair*)

Señor...

The Masked Man (*refusing*)

No. I

Would stand...

(*Aside*)

Will he, too, spurn and look awry
Upon me?

(*There is a moment of uncomfortable silence. Aloud, to Diégarias*)

You awaited someone?

Diégarias

Yes.
A friend.

(*There is another moment of silence.*)

The Masked Man

I come... In the king's name.

Diégarias (*coldly*)

No less
Did I suppose, señor.

(*Another silence*)

The Masked Man

I would suspect
You guess the message that he sends.

Diégarias

Correct...
Your master's hope is flown. He trembles lest
His throne be lost. And rightly so! East, west,
North, south... Rare is such unity upon
This soil! Cadiz, Navarre, and Aragon...
Valladolid, Olmedo... Yes, and other
Cities as well have joined with one another...
Proud Salamanca too!... And all support
The rebels who rise up against the court

And king!... Gold? Full their coffers! Much have they,
Señor!... Their army? One could almost say
It is invincible!... And, what is more,
Many at court have turned conspirator—
Commander, Admiral, His Majesty's
Archbishop too... And with them, if you please,
The people, ready to revolt whenever
Fright spurs them on... Now here, now there... Wherever...
And then Granada, of the loathing eye,
Waiting for him to perish, standing by,
Watching... And our Seville, as well, who moans
And groans, in loud lament, against the throne's
Excesses!... Add to all of that the bands
Of blackguard brigands wandering the land's
Expanse... Foul tide, remorseless, flooding all
The countryside... The cities, big and small...
Pillaging, looting...

The Masked Man (*aside*)

Ah! Alas...

Diégarias (*continuing*)

I would
Not paint in darker colors than I should.
But even if, indeed, we could forget
The scourges that are coming to beset
And plague us... Like the famine that, señor,
Wastes us already, and will do so more
And more... Pray, by what means will he dispel
His terrifying future? Can you tell
Me what resources has this king? Can he
Wage battle? No. Has he a coterie
Of powerful allies in Spain? No. Can
He count on soldiers, loyal to a man,
And who hold dear their flag, who glory in
Their honor, unalloyed, through thick and thin?
No, he can not.

The Masked Man (*aside*)

Ah!...

Diégarias (*continuing*)

I see many a brave
Captain, of noble race and name, behave
Disloyally, for whom the only thing
That keeps them in the service of the king
Is money! Their fidelity, I fear,
Comes with a price!

The Masked Man (*aside*)

Indeed!

Diégarias (*continuing*)

And it is dear,
Señor!

The Masked Man (*aside*)

He speaks the truth!

Diégarias (*continuing*)

So you can see
That strength, success, will, probability
Conspire against the powers of the crown.
Tomorrow, if an army should cast down
The gauntlet—in Seville, perhaps—how might
This king of yours resist? How would he fight?
Five thousand soldiers would he need... And then
A good six hundred archers... Hardy men,
Accustomed to pitched battle... Most of all,
Señor, would he require the wherewithal
To pay them!

The Masked Man

And you know the realm's finances!

Diégarias

I daresay!... Thus, under the circumstances,
Only one man possesses such a sum
To suit his need... Myself...

(*Archly*)

Now then, you come...

The Masked Man

For reasons that you must have guessed.

Diégarias

Indeed!

The Masked Man (*hesitating*)

And, may I ask... What then...

(*Aside*)

Ah! Will he heed
My plea? Or will he too abandon me?

(*Aloud*)

What is your answer?

Diégarias

So, His Majesty
Turns now to me, when one and all eschew
His royal presence, sure that I, the Jew,
Jacob Eliacin, myself alone,
Hold in my hands the future of the throne!
What? Is it so?

The Masked Man

Thus does he think, and such
Is his belief.

Diégarias

Thinks he not forasmuch,
That this... this Jew—bitter, cast out, laid low—
Might pay him tear for tear, and woe for woe?

The Masked Man (*hesitating*)

He hopes that, when his eyes perceive the plight
Of this, his country... our Castile... he might
Let the past lie in ruins.

Diégarias (*sarcastically*)

Mine, you say?
My country?

The Masked Man

We are all her children.

Diégarias

Eh?
Who would have thought! I think you must confess
That, in her haughty soul, much tenderness
Our mother has for some, and for the others,
Loathing! Not quite the tenderest of mothers,
Think you, señor?

The Masked Man

Please, sire... The question... I
Would know your answer. How do you reply?

Diégarias

Pray tell His Majesty that I agree.
But on condition.

The Masked Man (*surprised*)

On condition?

Diégarias (*still sarcastically*)

Be

Assured, I mean no disrespect! Nor do
I wish to make undue demands. But you
Surely can see that, at this time, señor,
There is, I fear, neither a master nor
A subject... Just two beings, each with a wish.
His Majesty's? The rather feverish
Desire for gold...

The Masked Man

And yours?

Diégarias

The count Don Juan
Is, as we speak, held prisoner. Thereupon
Hangs my condition. For it is my aim
To pay him for his crime, to cleanse the shame
He heaped upon me. Let the king arrange
A trade: his head, my gold! A fair exchange,
Think you not?

The Masked Man (*appalled*)

But... A grandee's blood! It would
Be base to traffic so!

Diégarias

My fatherhood,
Señor, and my good name demand that price
To wreak my vengeance. Naught less will suffice
Against the traitor who, I warrant, will
Not stop at one indignity!

The Masked Man

But still,

His life...

Diégarias

Revenge is my last joy. I said:
"A fair exchange... My gold for Don Juan's head!"
So be it. No more need I say.

The Masked Man (*aside*)

How low
Have I sunk, O misfortune, to be so
Reduced? I shudder! O Castile! O throne!
Passion for power! What sins will you condone
To feed my pride? What will you yet demand
Of me?

Diégarias

Señor, you hold within your hand
The future of the king.

The Masked Man

Your wish will be
Granted. You shall be satisfied.

Diégarias

And he
Shall die?

The Masked Man

Tomorrow.

Diégarias

We agree...

The Masked Man

You may

Come to the palace in one hour.

(*To the other Masked Man, in the background*)

You, stay

Here until then, and keep your watch.

(*He leaves. The other Masked Man bolts the door and approaches Diégarias. As he stands before him he removes his mask and reveals that he is Don Sanche.*)

Don Sanche (*to Diégarias*)

I must

Compliment you on your performance! Just
As it should be!

Diégarias (*surprised*)

Don Sanche!

SCENE 6

Diégarias, Don Sanche

Don Sanche

Well done, and very

Skillfully! With one blow—extraordinary!—
You find the means to take revenge on one
Whilst pardoning the other! Nobly done!

Diégarias (*coldly*)

Ah! Be not quite so quick, my friend, to twit
My plan! Better that you should speak of it
When you know more!

Don Sanche

You mean...?

Diégarias

I mean, I do
Not have a mind to banter here with you
And waste my precious time in idle chatter.
Now then, if I may ask... Our other matter,
Don Sanche?... Three days I waited, but there came
No one to see me... No López, by name!...
Then here you come...

(*Pointing to the door*)

With him... How can I be
Certain to trust you now?

Don Sanche

Each vis-à-vis
The other, sire...

Diégarias (*with a bitter smile*)

Aha! I see!... You mean,
Service for service?

Don Sanche

Quite! A trade between
Ourselves...

Diégarias

Indeed! An even tit for tat!

Don Sanche

So might you say. Surely you find not that
Surprising?

Diégarias

On the contrary! When kin
Do naught but for a price, what should, therein,

Be strange betwixt a Christian and a Jew?
So, let me hear your proposition.

Don Sanche

You
Surely must know that we intend to take
Advantage of Seville's unrest, and make
Her citizenry's cause our own. There stand
Ready a host of soldiers, many a band
Of men eager to fight the adversary.
But...

Diégarias

But?

Don Sanche

We feel it will be necessary
That, if success is going to smile upon
Our mission, we shall need the aid of Don
Guzmán, Seville's alcalde.

Diégarias

For a price,
No doubt!

Don Sanche

Alas!

Diégarias

What figure will entice
Him to your noble cause?

Don Sanche

He will demand
Three hundred thousand ducats, in his hand.

Diégarias

Then give him such!

Don Sanche

We have them not!

Diégarias

You will!

But only on condition that Seville
Rise up tomorrow! Let the crack of doom
Be heard throughout the land! Let fire consume
The foe at once!

Don Sanche

All is in readiness.

Diégarias (*growing more and more impassioned*)

Then am I with you! And not one whit less
Than any other! Yes, this very day
I pledge my faith before God... My God... Yea,
The father!

(*Raising his eyes to heaven*)

You who see and hear my prayer!
And you, O boundless stars and planets! Bear
Witness to my sincerity!... Were all
The thunderbolts of heaven at once to fall
Upon my head... Were I to feel the wrath
And fury blaring in the tempest's path...
Were I to be consumed by lions... Still
Would I pledge all my heart, my mind, my will
To this rebellion!... Ah! This king shall find
In me... This king, whom anarchy shall bind
Tight in its chains, shall find in me, I vow,
Nothing but utter hate and vengeance!

(*To Don Sanche*)

Now
Must I begone!

Don Sanche

Whereto?

Diégarias

Best I repair
Presently to the palace. It is there
That I belong, not here.

Don Sanche

But is that wise?
You know, old man, that when the king lays eyes
Upon you... Gone your gold, and off your head!

Diégarias

I only know time walks with heavy tread
Upon my life, and that shame and disgrace
Cast a foul shadow, plodding on apace,
Upon that old man's hoary head, grown white
With woe!

Don Sanche

But know you not the deathly plight
Awaiting you?

Diégarias (*impassioned*)

What matters that? My one
And only wish is that my will be done!
If die I must, let me, with my last breath,
Savor my vengeance, as, whisked to their death,

They die as well! Then shall I die content!
The villains shall have had their punishment!

(*Inès enters.*)

SCENE 7

Inès, Diégarias, Don Sanche, upstage, in the background.

Inès (*to Diégarias*)

Father, an envoy from His Majesty
Would speak with you...

Diégarias (*turning round, to Inès*)

Ah, you, my child...

(*Drawing her to him*)

Come... Be
Not sad, Inès!... Hold high your head! Be proud!
Many a day have we spent, bent and bowed
By fortune. But, soon, blood will wash our tears.
This is no empty hope. The moment nears
When vengeance will be ours! With steady pace
And sure, I march to the appointed place,
And to the final hour that both of them
Will ever see!

Inès

Both...?

Diégarias

Yes.

(*Holding out his hands*)

These hands condemn
Both of them to the death their infamy
Deserves!

Inès

Them...? Both...? But... Who...

Diégarias

His Majesty
And—

Inès (*quickly, suspecting*)

And...?

Diégarias

The count.

Inès (*visibly shaken, leaning against a chair*)

The count?

Diégarias (*without noticing her distress*)

Yes. As we speak,
They build the very scaffold that will wreak
Your vengeance on him! Thus will he, like us,
Be cast down from his lofty, glorious
Pinnacle, to the depths!...

(*Finally noticing her reaction*)

Inès! You grow
Pale! What is it! Why do you tremble so?
What ails you?... Tell me...

Inès (*unable to control her emotion*)

Ails me, father?... Now
Shall you call down your wrath upon my brow!
Now must you learn... Now must my tongue confess

That when, at first, I felt the wretchedness,
The bitterness of my condition, sore
Distressed was I... So deep the wound I bore,
That, in my pain, I asked you... Oh! I pled,
Swore that I wished you to...

(*Struggling against her recollection*)

No, no! I dread
Even to think that I... But does the heart
Weigh out the words our miseries impart
And dictate to our tongues?... So great my grief,
So deep...

Diégarias

Inès...

Inès (*continuing*)

That I sought its relief
In blood! Yes, I implored you to restore
My honor with his death!... Ah, but no more!

Diégarias

What?

Inès

Ah! You ought have seen that I had taken
Leave of my senses!... That I had forsaken
My very soul! Alas! I said what rose
Trippingly to my lips... Good God! In those
Moments of hopelessness who knows what thought
Our tongues express? We say what our distraught,
Unthinking minds propose...

Diégarias

But he—

Inès (*continuing*)

I must
Confess that he who shook, shattered my trust,
Whose love dishonored, sullied me, until
I sought his death... Alas, I love him still.

Diégarias
Inès!

Inès (*throwing herself at his feet*)
I beg you, father! One last word...
Mercy! Oh, mercy! Let your heart be stirred
To pity! Kill him not!... In heaven's name,
I beg you!... Ah! I know the horrid shame
I suffered at his hands. And yet, although
My pride demands that I abhor him... No,
I cannot!... Little do you know to what
Lengths folly spurs us, drives us on! Should not
I hate the very sight of him?... Oh, how
I wish I could! How I would disavow
The coward!... Nay, the odious wretch, who, turning
My future to his plaything, toying, spurning
My love, destroyed my honor!... Welladay!
Good God! I love him! What more can I say?

Diégarias (*trying to control his emotion*)
Alas! Another woe to weigh on me!

(*He goes to leave.*)

Inès (*reaching out to him*)
Please, father...

(*Almost swooning with grief, as Diégarias, without replying, leaves*)

No... I pray...

SCENE 8

Inès (*alone, recovering her senses*)

Ah, misery!
The scaffold... Oh! To think... To see him there,
Hanging above death's deep abyss... Aware
That I am powerless...

(*Raising her arms to heaven*)

O God! Be kind!
Pity my plight...

(*Noticing a parchment that, in her emotion, has fallen from her bosom*)

What...?

(*Examining it*)

This... It...

(*Realizing what it is*)

Ah! Sealed, signed...
The king's carte blanche!

(*Recalling The King's statement to her*)

"Inès, I place his fate
Into your hands!..."

(*Joyously*)

Then is it not too late!

(*After writing several words on the parchment*)

O heart of mine, hope is not dead. For I
Will save his life! Count Don Juan shall not die!

CURTAIN

Act 5

A dimly lit prison. Upstage, a large door. Stage right, a small door. Stage left, a barred window. Stage right, a table with a chair and a lamp. Downstage, a bench. A crucifix on one of the walls.

SCENE I

Don Juan is half-sitting, half-lying on the bench. The Jailer is in the background, leaning against the door.

Don Juan (*musing*)
No doubt the king is pleased that he possesses
A prison in the palace's recesses
Dismal as this, with warders that could be
No uglier!...

(*Lying out*)

Come, sleep! Deliver me
To sweet oblivion!...

(*The sounds of hammering can be heard outside.*)

Damn!... Not again!
Is there no end to it?

(*To The Jailer*)

What do those men
Outside the walls?

The Jailer (*reluctantly*)
Oh... Nothing.

Don Juan

Must they make
Such noise for nothing?... Do my ears mistake,
Or are they building something?

The Jailer

Building...? No...

Don Juan

Go look!

(*The Jailer does not move. Don Juan repeats, commanding*)

Go look, I said! Why tarry so?
You were my lackey once! If now no more
You are, still...

The Jailer (*sadly, pointing to the window*)

But... Look for yourself, señor...

Don Juan

Quite right!...

(*He goes to the window and looks out.*)

A scaffold!

(*To The Jailer, after a moment of silence*)

Is it then today?
So soon?

The Jailer (*aside*)

Alas!

Don Juan

Tell me!

The Jailer (*sadly*)

What can I say?
God is your only hope.

(*Don Juan stands silently contemplating the scaffold.*)

Don Juan

Ah! Look at it!
His Majesty does me the exquisite
Honor of building me a new one! Most
Gallant and proper of my royal host!

(*After another silence, to The Jailer*)

How shall I leave?

The Jailer (*pointing upstage*)

The corridor... Then out
Into the courtyard...

Don Juan

So... Today, no doubt?
This morning?

The Jailer

Eight o'clock.

Don Juan

I see...

The Jailer

Señor...

Don Juan

Leave!... I would be alone!

(*As The Jailer leaves, a clock begins striking. Don Juan counts.*)

One... Two... Three... Four...

(*The clock strikes three more times as Don Juan counts in silence.*)

Seven o'clock... Well then, I yet have time...

SCENE 2

Don Juan (*alone, sitting down*)
Another hour, perforce, before I climb
Up to the scaffold! Ah! who would have thought...?
What have I done with life? What have I wrought
With these my thirty years? When I appear
At Satan's feet, only one thing, I fear,
Shall I remember... Something that now gnaws
My heart... Inès's memory!... Because,
For all the ill I did that pure, sweet child,
Deeply have I repented and reviled
My deed!

(*He remains absorbed in his reflections. The upstage door opens and The Jailer, holding a parchment, enters, showing in Inès, heavily veiled, followed by Pérez.*)

SCENE 3
Don Juan, Inès, The Jailer, Pérez

The Jailer (*to Inès*)
Enter, señora... You were sent
By God!

(*Inès removes her veil and gestures to Pérez to wait at the door. The Jailer approaches Don Juan, excitedly.*)

Count!... Count!... The king, omnipotent,
Has pardoned you!

Don Juan (*roused from his reverie, not believing his ears*)
The king?... He...

The Jailer (*waving the parchment*)
Yes! You see?

(*Giving it to him*)

His seal! You know it!

Inès (*approaching Don Juan, still unseen by him*)
Yes! By his decree,
His Majesty has done for you, Don Juan,
What he has never done for anyone
Before. He pardons you.

Don Juan (*turning round, seeing her*)
My God!... You!... How—

Inès (*interrupting him, continuing*)
But only if you quit his realm, and vow
Not to return!

Don Juan
Inès—

Inès
Now, quickly! Go!
Begone!

Don Juan (*deeply moved*)
So! It is you who save me!... O
Inès!... Despite my past... Can it be true?
Despite my base offense, yet would you do
This sublime deed! Such is the price you pay
For my disgrace!

(*Falling at her feet*)

Oh, pardon! Pardon, pray,
My infamy! I beg... beseech you...

Inès

Please,
Señor!...

Don Juan (*supplicating*)

Pardon!... Forgive me! On my knees,
Inès...

Inès (*with a gesture*)

Rise! Rise, count!

Don Juan (*rising to his feet*)

Understand you not
Why now I tremble? Why the tears roll hot
Upon my cheek?... Look not upon me here
As that brash rogue, the brazen cavalier
That once I was!... That churl, whose soul stood shut
To thought of honor!... Yes, such was I. But
No more, Inès!... I know not what wrought this
Change in my life, this metamorphosis...
But suddenly my heart grows pure, my whole
Being springs anew, unto my very soul!
Before your selfless grandeur I discover
That he who was a liar... is now a lover.

Inès (*coldly*)

I did not hope to gain this victory,
Señor. And, surely, it will ever be
A source of pleasure, graven deeply in
My memory. But, though I gladly win
A place within your heart, I must admit,
Your gratitude is needless: not a whit

Is it for you that I do what I do,
But for myself. For I, count, in God's view,
Have been, and am, your rightful wife. It is
Duty, señor, that makes me act in His—
And my—behalf, not yours.

Don Juan

Ah! If I dare
Speak to you of my love, it is, I swear,
Because repentance raises loud its voice...
Because, at last, my heart and soul rejoice
In my redemption!... Yea, because my crime
Will have its punishment! Though brief my time,
I am content. And so I must reject
This pardon that you bring, else no respect
Would I have for the life you save. My past
Demands my death.

Inès

But count...

Don Juan

Blithely I cast
My scorn upon the faith you pledged... With no
Remorse, I treated you as would a low,
Impudent wretch... Unworthy, cowardly...
Worse yet, I stole your honor and made free
With my disdain! Alas, I should have knelt
Down at your feet in love! Instead, I dealt
You naught but woe! You can, perhaps, with your
Sublime compassion, pardon me, the poor
Sinner I used to be... But I would never
Forget my crime. It would haunt me forever,
And be a lasting chastisement.

Inès

But—

Don Juan

No,

After what I have done, I would not owe
My life, Inès, to pity! Sinned have I
Against your love, and I deserve to die!

Inès (*very agitated*)

But why... Who said that I... Wherefore do you
Think that I do for pity what I do?
What of my tears, señor? Do I berate
You for them, or... or for my hopeless state?
Please! If your tongue speaks true... If you repent...
If anything I say can yet prevent
Your folly... Please, count! Go! And quickly!... For...
If you should die, I could not live, señor!...
I love you!

Don Juan (*controlling his emotion*)

Ah!... Then go I shall.

Inès (*taking him by the hand, as if to move upstage*)

Come!... Here...

Don Juan (*stopping, with deep sincerity*)

So! I am free? And I may leave this drear
And somber prison? And you ask of me
Naught in return? My word? My guarantee?
Nothing?... Still, I upon my brow shall wear
Ever the traitor's mark, emblazoned there
For all the cruel perversity of my
Sin before God!... But now I swear hereby,
Before Him...

(*Pointing to the crucifix*)

and the image of the Christ—
This image of the savior sacrificed—

I swear that, be you Jewess, be you not,
Whoever be the forebears that begot
And nurtured you... I swear that, if you deign
Let your eyes look upon my face again,
Washed clean will be the shame I bear today,
And you shall be my countess!

Inès (*without listening, pulling him toward the door, upstage*)

Yes... This way,
Count!... Please!...

Pérez (*to Don Juan*)

Come, sire...

Don Juan (*at the door*)

Inès... Ah! My Inès...
Until we meet again...

(*Kissing her hand*)

Farewell!

Inès

Ah, yes...

(*Sadly*)

Farewell, Don Juan...

(*Pérez pulls Don Juan out the door, and they leave.*)

SCENE 4
Inès, then The Jailer

Inès (*alone*)

Forever...

(*She remains silent for a moment, then comes downstage.*)

Have I spared
My executioner?... What? Have I dared
Commit this treason? This... this felony!...
Yes? No?... Alas! What matters it to me?
He shall be free, and I... I shall be dead.

(*Removing a phial from her bosom, holding it up*)

My punishment!... And well deserved!

(*Contemplating the phial*)

What dread
Death for a Christian soul! Foul poison!... Oh,
But is there any misery or woe
Equal to mine?

(*She remains deep in contemplation as The Jailer enters.*)

The Jailer

Señora, please! You stay
Too long!

Inès (*rousing herself*)

I know!

(*Sadly*)

No more...

(*She replaces the phial and prepares to follow him. As The Jailer opens the door, Diégarias appears. Inès moves quickly to one side.*)

God!

SCENE 5

Diégarias, Inès, The Jailer

Diégarias (*to The Jailer*)

You!... You may
Give me the prisoner, on the king's demand!

(*Showing him a document*)

Here is the order!... Quickly! Understand?
Time presses!

The Jailer (*confused*)

But, the count... He has been freed!

Diégarias (*appalled*)

Freed? Are you mad?

The Jailer

No, sire. The king decreed
His pardon...

(*Showing him the parchment*)

Here and now...

Diégarias (*beside himself*)

What say you, swine?

(*He peruses the parchment, then flings it down, trampling it.*)

Hell and damnation!

(*Waving the king's order under his nose*)

Look! See you his sign?...

His signature?... The royal crest?... This order
Comes from the king!

(*Growing more and more outraged*)

Cursed be the dungeon warder
Who lets himself be duped! Or who conspires
To free his prisoner!

The Jailer

But—

Diégarias

By all hell's fires,
You shall be punished!

The Jailer (*picking up the parchment, holding it out*)

But... His Majesty...
He signed this pardon! Do you not agree,
Sire?

Diégarias (*furiously*)

No! He signed it not!

The Jailer

The seal...

Diégarias

No, lout!

(*Emphatically*)

He signed it not!

The Jailer

Ah, then! There is no doubt!

(*Pointing to Inès, cowering, veiled, in the shadow*)

That woman... She who stands there, veiled and trembling...
She it was, who, I fear, by her dissembling,
Wrought the fell deed! She must not leave! The king
Shall learn at once of her maneuvering...

(*He leaves hurriedly.*)

SCENE 6

Diégarias, Inès, veiled.

Inès (*aside*)
God help me!

Diégarias (*looking at her, aside*)
Who...? A woman?... What? Could it...?
What horrible suspicion... Have I quit
My senses?... But, Inès? How could it...

(*Relieved*)

Bah!
She left this very day for Alcalá.
I took her there myself!

(*To Inès, approaching*)

Pray you... Your name,
Señora?

Inès (*falling at his feet*)
One that I have cast great shame
Upon!

Diégarias (*lifting her veil*)
My God! It is!... Inès!

Inès

Please, vent
Your wrath upon me, sire! No punishment
Is harsh enough, wretched enough for one
Who, in her grief, has done what I have done.

Diégarias (*struggling to contain himself*)
Stand up! Fall not again upon your knees!

(*Lifting her up, sharply*)

Up! Up, I tell you!

(*He pauses.*)

So, the scoundrel flees!
Where? By which road?

Inès (*pathetically*)

Father...

Diégarias

No tears! No cries
Of anguish, please! I want the truth! No lies,
No vain regrets!... Now must you choose betwixt
Father and lover!

(*After a pause, as Inès remains silent, eyes downcast*)

Well? Stand not transfixed!

Inès (*wringing her hands*)
But sire...

Diégarias

Be quick! Reply!

Inès

You ask of me
A choice unequaled in its cruelty!
How—

Diégarias (*interrupting her, sharply*)

You decide! Abandon him, unless
You would no longer be my child, Inès!

Inès

Mercy! I beg you!

Diégarias

Which road did he take?
Reply!

Inès

How can you ask that I forsake
This man?

Diégarias

He is the cause of all our woe!

Inès

Ah! But I love him. That is all I know.

Diégarias

And I know only that your lips refuse
To speak!

Inès

Punish me any way you choose,
Father! But I can not... will not betray
The same poor soul I dared to save this day!

Diégarias (*scornfully*)

Indeed! Alas, I could have... should have guessed

How such as you would honor my request!
No! Fate has spoken!

Inès

Father...

Diégarias

And its voice
Has, by your silence, proclaimed loud your choice,
Inès!

Inès

Please, scorn me not! I cannot stand
To hear you thus rebuke and reprimand
A daughter who so loves you! I am surely
Not one of those who, with false tears, demurely,
Dare to conceal their shameless perfidy.
If ever father were loved, honored, he
Never could be so any more than you.
What I did, sire, was what I had to do!
If, suddenly, I let this one offense,
With bitter tears, shake the obedience
That, lo! these many years, has been respected...
Ah, pray, let me not be despised, rejected
Because I could not follow your commands.
I beg you! Raise not now your loving hands
To curse me! It were foul and blasphemous,
Father, for any honest woman, thus
Shamefully to betray her lover. Nay,
Make me not add another sin, I pray,
To those that weigh upon me!

(*Diégarias looks away.*)

Ah! You turn
Aside?... You would not listen?... Please, sire! Spurn

Not my entreaty... You, who must know all
The pangs of love... Who must, yourself, recall
Its power and pain!... Long years ago, in spite
Of all the perils of a headlong flight
To live beneath a foreign sky, in other
Climes than her own, unknown... Ah! If my mother—

Diégarias
Be still!

Inès (*continuing*)
If she, Bianca, your wife, had seen
Love pale for him whose mistress she had been,
And if her waning passion had betrayed
His trust, abandoned him, and disobeyed
Honor's demands... I am afraid that it
Would have been sinful! Sire, you must admit...
For, if the guilty ravisher were taken,
The husband, likewise, would have been forsaken...
You, sire—

Diégarias
Be still! Be still!

Inès (*throwing herself at his feet*)
You are a good,
Kind, gentle soul! And never, never would
You be without compassion! Pray think of
Our happy past. Think of the tender love
My mother felt for you... She who looks, now,
Down from above, and sees me here... Think how
Pleased she would be to see you pardon me!
Mercy!

(*Diégarias, visibly shaken, seems about to relent. The Jailer has entered on the last few words.*)

SCENE 7
Inès, Diégarias, The Jailer

The Jailer

Too late! Alas, he could not flee
Even unto the city walls!

Inès (trembling, to The Jailer)

Don Juan?

The Jailer

Yes. He was captured, and stands now upon
The scaffold, as I speak!

Inès (faintly)

Oh...

The Jailer

Listen well...

A Voice (outside, proclaiming)

"... Don Juan de Tello, count of Santafiel,
Grandee, lord of La Rueda, is hereby
Guilty of treason, and condemned to die.
Pray for his soul."

Inès (pathetically, raising her arms to heaven)

No, God! I beg you!... No!

The Voice (outside)

Justice is done!

Inès (shattered, mournfully)

And so the final blow
Is struck. And so it ends. Soon will they pray
Not for one soul, but two... I go my way

Unto the tomb, that, unrelentingly,
Draws me to him, and him, at last, to me.

(*Taking the phial from her bosom*)

For, those the scaffold cruelly rends apart,
This draught joins, soul to soul, and heart to heart.

(*She drinks the poison, unseen by Diégarias, who has remained prostrate. The King enters.*)

SCENE 8

Diégarias, The King, Inès, then The Inquisitor, Grandees, Guards

The King (*brusquely, to Diégarias*)
Don Juan is dead.

Diégarias (*raising his head, weakly*)
Your Majesty...?

The King
Now then...
My promise has been kept. One of my men
Informs me that you made one too. Now will
You keep it!

Inès (*beside herself with grief, approaching him, boldly*)
O great monarch! You who kill,
Then dare to claim, unbowed, the service bought
With death, and to survey the mourning wrought
Upon your hopeless victim!

(*Looking at Diégarias*)

You...

(*Looking at The King*)

And you...

(*Pointing at him, disdainfully*)

What can repair... repay the ill you two...

(*Sarcastically*)

O king revered, worshipped, beloved!... Who wears
With pride the regal crown, boldly declares
Himself above affront... Go look behind
The royal purple, never will you find
A soul more blackened by the fires of hell!
Go look beneath his mantle!... Yes, look well!
There will you see not strength, but blood!

The King (*to Inès*)

I fear
Your grief makes you forget, Inès my dear,
That I—

Inès (*growing weaker*)
Threaten me not... I am above
Your threats... But tell me, where... Where is the love,
The husband that you gave me?

(*She pauses briefly.*)

Why reply?
You know, O noble king, as well as I,
That you have killed him for a sack of gold!

The King (*to Diégarias, angrily*)
What does she know?

Diégarias

She knows that you have sold...
You, in whose lofty, kingly veins, there flows
The blood of ages past, and of all those
Proud sires of old... You, who command the reins
Of empire, and who—so your fate ordains—
Ought not aspire but to the highest goal...
Yes, yes. She knows that you have sold your soul
And all your subjects' blood, for gold!

The King (*aside*)

Disaster!

Diégarias (*with disdain*)

Let be whatever will, O royal master!
Let me be drawn and quartered... Let me be
Dismembered, and my limbs hung shamefully
Upon the city's walls! No matter! My
Vengeance is done! Contented can I die,
Now that you are brought down!

The King (*shouting*)

Guards! Guards!

Diégarias

Call them!
What care I now?

(*Two Guards appear. A bell rings in the distance.*)

Soon shall your requiem
Be sung! Your time is come! Your knell has tolled...
The dwarf becomes a giant!

The King (*despairing*)

Ah...

(*Flames begin reflecting on the walls.*)

Diégarias (*pointing to the flickering reflections*)
Behold!

Inès (*upstage, slumping, aside*)
How slow my poison!... God!

The King (*to Diégarias, terrified*)
Whence come those flames?

Where...?

Inès (*dying*)
Ah, Don Juan... I join you...

(*She falls over, dead.*)

Diégarias (*unaware of Inès, to The King, triumphantly*)
All your shames,
And sins, and crimes burn in one conflagration!
Each tongue of flame shrieks cries of expiation
Unto your very soul!

The King
But how... The fires—

Diégarias (*interrupting*)
Are proof that all Seville rises, conspires
Against you! The rebellion is at hand!

The King (*shouting*)
Wretch!

Diégarias (*joyously*)
Do you hear the noise throughout the land?
The deep, dark rumble of the storm?... The thunder,
Growling, grumbling, wrenching the night asunder?

The King (*aghast*)
Oh!

Diégarias (*growing more and more impassioned*)
Yes, it is the people that you hear!
The sovereign people, who will persevere
Until, burning with rage, with arms of steel
Entwining you, they crush you, make you feel
Their rightful wrath, trample your crown, destroy
Your throne, whose scraps, bits, in a fit of joy,
They will refashion in a coffin for
Your royal bones!... Give ear! That mighty roar
You hear... It is the people, with one voice,
Crying out for a ruler of their choice!
Resign yourself, prince of the blood! A Jew
Has smashed the throne for all who follow you!

(*The Inquisitor enters hurriedly, along with several Grandees.*)

The Inquisitor (*to The King*)
Your Majesty, the rebels have our forts.
Don Sanche it is who, with his vile cohorts,
Urges them on. Resistance is of no
Avail!... No!... Flee you must, and quickly! Though
The cause is lost, perhaps Your Majesty
Can save himself and, one day, possibly,
Restore the empire and the crown!

The King (*enraged, to Diégarias*)
Ah, you!...

(*To The Inquisitor*)

One moment! I have business first!

(*To The Guards*)

You two...

(*Pointing to Diégarias*)

Seize him!

(*To Diégarias*)

Though my delay might cost my flight,
Yet shall I pay you for your crime, this blight
Upon my royal name!

(*To The Guards*)

Seize him, I say!

(*Pointing to Inès*)

And her!

(*To one of The Grandees*)

Arrest them both!

Diégarias

Inès?

The King (*to The Grandee*)

Obey,
Don Diegue!

Diégarias (*turning round, suddenly seeing Inès lying motionless, gasping*)
Dear God! Let my eyes be beguiled!...

(*Running over to her, placing his hand on her breast. In despair*)

I sought revenge...

(*Falling on her body*)

But I have killed my child!

CURTAIN

Suggestions for Further Reading

Antier, Benjamin, and Alex Decomberousse. *Le Marché de Saint-Pierre.* Paris: Marchant, 1839.

Beaumarchais, Jean-Paul de, Daniel Couty, and Alain Rey. *Dictionnaire des littératures de langue française.* Rev. ed. Paris: Bordas, 1994.

Bell, Caryn Cossé. *Revolution, Romanticism, and the Afro-Creole Protest Tradition in Louisiana, 1718–1868.* Baton Rouge: Louisiana State University Press, 1997.

Blassingame, John. *Black New Orleans, 1860–1880.* Chicago: University of Chicago Press, 1973.

Bongie, Chris. *Islands and Exiles: The Creole Identities of Post/Colonial Literature.* Stanford: Stanford University Press, 1998.

Boucicault, Dion. *The Octoroon.* 1859. Reprint. New Jersey: Literature House, 1970.

Brisbane, Era Mae. "Théatre de Victor Séjour." M.A. thesis, Hunter College, 1942.

Les Cenelles: A Collection of Poems by Creole Writers of the Early Nineteenth Century. Translated by Régine Latortue and Gleason R. W. Adams. Boston: G. K. Hall, 1979.

Coleman, Edward Maceo. *Creole Voices: Poems in French by Free Men of Color First Published in 1845.* Washington, D.C.: Associated Publishers, 1945.

Cottin, John Richard. "Victor Séjour: Sa vie et son théâtre." Ph.D. diss., University of Montreal, 1957.

Daley, T. A. "Victor Séjour." *Phylon* 4 (1943): 5–15.

Davidson, James Woods. *Living Writers of the South.* New York, 1869.

Desdunes, Rodolphe. *Our People and Our History.* Baton Rouge: Louisiana State University Press, 1973.

Fabre, Michel. "New Orleans Creole Expatriates in France: Romance and

Reality." In *Creole: The History and Legacy of Louisiana's Free People of Color*, ed. Sybil Kein. Baton Rouge: Louisana State University Press, 2000.

———. "International Beacons of African-American Memory: Alexandre Dumas Père, Henry O. Tanner, and Josephine Baker as Examples of Recognition." In *History and Memory in African-American Culture*, ed. Geneviève Fabre and Robert O'Meally. New York: Oxford University Press, 1994.

———. *From Harlem to Paris: American Writers in France, 1840–1980*. Urbana: University of Illinois Press, 1991.

Gates, Henry Louis, and Nellie McKay. *The Norton Anthology of African-American Literature.* New York: W. W. Norton, 1997.

Hatch, James, and Ted Shine, eds. *Black Theatre USA: Plays by African Americans.* Vol. 1: *The Early Period: 1847–1938.* New York: Free Press, 1996.

Hemmings, F. W. J. *The Theatre Industry in Nineteenth-Century France.* Cambridge: Cambridge University Press, 1993.

Hoffmann, Léon-François. *Le nègre romantique: personnage littéraire et obsession collective.* Paris: Payot, 1973.

Kein, Sybil. *Creole: The History and Legacy of Louisiana's Free People of Color.* Baton Rouge: Louisiana State University Press, 2000.

McCormick, John. *Popular Theatres of Nineteenth-Century France.* London: Routledge, 1993.

O'Connell, David. "Victor Séjour: Ecrivain Américain de Langue Française." *Revue de Louisiane* 1 (Winter 1972): 60–61.

O'Neill, Charles Edwards. *Séjour: Parisian Playwright from Louisiana.* Lafayette: Center for Louisiana Studies, University of Southwestern Louisiana, 1995.

———. "Theatrical Censorship in France, 1844–1875: The Experience of Victor Séjour." *Harvard Library Bulletin* 26 (1978): 417–41.

Perret, John. "Victor Séjour, Black French Playwright from Louisiana." *Teachers of French* 57 (Dec. 1983): 187–93.

Reybaud, Mme. Charles. *Valdepeiras.* Paris: Hachette, 1864.

Roussève, Charles Barthelemy. *The Negro in Louisiana: Aspects of His History and His Literature.* 1937. Reprint, New York: Johnson Reprint Corporation, 1970.

Savard, Félix. "M. Victor Séjour." *La chronique littéraire* 2 (June 1862): 48–55.

Séjour, Victor. *La Tireuse de cartes.* Paris: Michel Levy Frères, 1860.

———. *Le Paletot brun.* Paris: Michel Levy Frères, 1859.

———. *Diégarias.* Paris: C. Tresse, 1844.

———. "Le Retour de Napoléon." Paris, 1841.

———. "Le Mulâtre." 1837. *Revue des colonies* 3 (Mar. 1837): 376–92.

Sollors, Werner. *Neither Black nor White yet Both: Thematic Explorations of Interracial Literature.* New York: Oxford University Press, 1997.

———. "'Never Was Born:' The Mulatto, an American Tragedy?" *Massachusetts Review* (Summer 1986): 293–316.

Tinker, Edward Laroque. *Les Ecrits de langue française en Louisiane au XIXe siècle.* Paris: Librarie Ancienne Honoré Champion, 1932.

———. *Les Cenelles: Afro-French Poetry in Louisiana.* New York: Spiral Press, 1930.

Viatte, Auguste. *Histoire littéraire de l'Amérique francaise des origines à 1950.* Paris: Presses universitaires de France, 1954.

Young Brisbane, Era. "An Examination of Selected Dramas of Victor Séjour including Works of Social Protest." Ph.D. diss., New York University, 1979.

Victor Séjour was born a free man of color in New Orleans in 1817. He left his native city at the age of nineteen for Paris, where he began a writing career. In 1837, Séjour published "The Mulatto," the first short story written by an African American. The Comédie Française performed *Diégarias* (*The Jew of Seville*), his first play, when Séjour was just twenty-six years old. Twenty of his twenty-two plays were performed in Paris and New Orleans between 1844 and 1875. Victor Séjour died in 1874 and is buried in Paris.

Norman R. Shapiro, professor of Romance languages and literatures at Wesleyan University, is a widely published translator of French poetry, prose, and theater. Among his works are *Four Farces of Georges Feydeau* (NBA nominee), *Fifty Fables of La Fontaine, The Fabulists French: Verse Fables of Nine Centuries* (ALTA Distinguished Book of the Year), *Selected Poems from "Les Fleurs du mal,"* and *One Hundred and One Poems of Paul Verlaine* (recent recipient of the MLA Scaglione Prize).

M. Lynn Weiss is an associate professor in American studies at the College of William and Mary. She is the author of *Gertrude Stein, Richard Wright: The Poetics and Politics of Modernism* (1998). Her more recent work is on Louisiana's Creoles of color.

The University of Illinois Press
is a founding member of the
Association of American University Presses.

Composed in 10.5/13 Adobe Caslon
with Berkeley display
by Barbara Evans
at the University of Illinois Press
Designed by Paula Newcomb
Manufactured by Thomson-Shore, Inc.

University of Illinois Press
1325 South Oak Street
Champaign, IL 61820-6903
www.press.uillinois.edu